MICROSOFT® OFFICE WORD® 2007

GREGG

College Keyboarding & Document Processing

OBER
JOHNSON
ZIMMERLY

MAP

Lessons 1-120
10th Edition

Higher Education

Boston   Burr Ridge, IL   Dubuque, IA   Madison, WI   New York   San Francisco   St. Louis
Bangkok   Bogotá   Caracas   Kuala Lumpur   Lisbon   London   Madrid   Mexico City
Milan   Montreal   New Delhi   Santiago   Seoul   Singapore   Sydney   Taipei   Toronto

McGraw-Hill
Higher Education

MICROSOFT® OFFICE WORD® 2007 MANUAL FOR GREGG COLLEGE KEYBOARDING &
DOCUMENT PROCESSING
Published by McGraw-Hill, a business unit of The McGraw-Hill Companies, Inc., 1221 Avenue of the
Americas, New York, NY, 10020.

This book is printed on acid-free paper.

3   4   5   6   7   8   9   0   CUS/CUS   0   9   8

ISBN   978-0-07-336835-1
MHID   0-07-336835-0

Vice President/Editor in Chief: *Elizabeth Haefele*
Vice President/Director of Marketing: *John E. Biernat*
Developmental editor: *Alaina Grayson*
Marketing manager: *Keari Bedford*
Marketing manager: *Megan Gates*
Lead media producer: *Damian Moshak*
Media producer: *Benjamin Curless*
Director, Editing/Design/Production: *Jess Ann Kosic*
Project manager: *Marlena Pechan*
Freelance project manager: *Rebecca Komro*
Senior production supervisor: *Janean A. Utley*
Designer: *Marianna Kinigakis*
Media project manager: *Mark Dierker*
Typeface: *11/12 Times Roman*
Compositor: *Aptara*
Printer: *R. R. Donnelley*

www.mhhe.com

CONTENTS

Reference Manual

COMPUTER SYSTEM

keyboard, R-2B
parts of, R-2A

CORRESPONDENCE

application letter, R-12B
attachment notation, R-4D
blind copy notation, R-5B
block style, R-3A
body, R-3A
company name, R-5B
complimentary closing, R-3A
copy notation, R-3C, R-5B
date line, R-3A
delivery notation, R-4A, R-5B
e-mail, R-5C-D
enclosure notation, R-3B, R-5B
envelope formatting, R-6A
executive stationery, R-4A
half-page stationery, R-4B
inside address, R-3A
international address, R-3D
letter folding, R-6B
letterhead, R-3A
lists, R-3B-C, R-12C-D
memo, R-4D
modified-block style, R-3B
multipage, R-5A-B
on-arrival notation, R-5A
open punctuation, R-3B
page number, R-5B
personal-business, R-3D
postscript notation, R-5B
reference initials, R-3A, R-5B
return address, R-3D
salutation, R-3A
simplified style, R-3C
standard punctuation, R-3A, R-3D
subject line, R-3C, R-5A, R-7C
table, R-4D
window envelope, folding for, R-6B
window envelope, formatted for, R-4C
writer's identification, R-3A

EMPLOYMENT DOCUMENTS

application letter, R-12B
resume, R-12A

FORMS

R-14A

LANGUAGE ARTS

abbreviations, R-22
adjectives and adverbs, R-20
agreement, R-19
apostrophes, R-17
capitalization, R-21
colons, R-18
commas, R-15 to R-16
grammar, R-19 to R-20
hyphens, R-17
italics (or underline), R-18
mechanics, R-21 to R-22
number expression, R-21 to R-22
periods, R-18
pronouns, R-20
punctuation, R-15 to R-18
quotation marks, R-18
semicolons, R-16
sentences, R-19
underline (or italics), R-18
word usage, R-20

PROOFREADERS' MARKS

R-14C

REPORTS

academic style, R-8C-D
agenda, R-11A
APA style, R-10A-B
author/year citations, R-10A
bibliography, R-9B
business style, R-8A-B, R-9A
byline, R-8A
citations, R-9D
date, R-8A
endnotes, R-8C-D
footnotes, R-8A-B
headings, R-9D

headings, paragraph, R-8A
headings, side, R-8A
itinerary, R-11C
left-bound, R-9A
legal document, R-11D
lists, R-8A, R-8C, R-12D
margins, R-9D
memo report, R-9C
minutes of a meeting, R-11B
MLA style, R-10C-D
outline, R-7A
quotation, long, R-8B, R-8D
references page, R-10B
resume, R-12A
spacing, R-9D
subtitle, R-8A
table, R-8B
table of contents, R-7D
title, R-8A
title page, R-7B
transmittal memo, R-7C
works-cited page, R-10D

TABLES

2-line column heading, R-13B
body, R-13A
boxed, R-13A
capitalization in columns, R-13D
column headings, R-13A-D
in correspondence, R-4D, R-5A
dollar signs, R-13D
heading block, R-13D
note, R-13A
open, R-13B
percent signs, R-13D
in reports, R-8B, R-13C
ruled, R-13C
subtitle, R-13A, R-13D
table number, R-13C
table source, R-8B
title, R-13A
total line, R-13A, R13-D
vertical placement, R-13D

U.S. POSTAL SERVICE STATE ABBREVIATIONS

R-14B

Reference Manual

A. MAJOR PARTS OF A MICROCOMPUTER SYSTEM

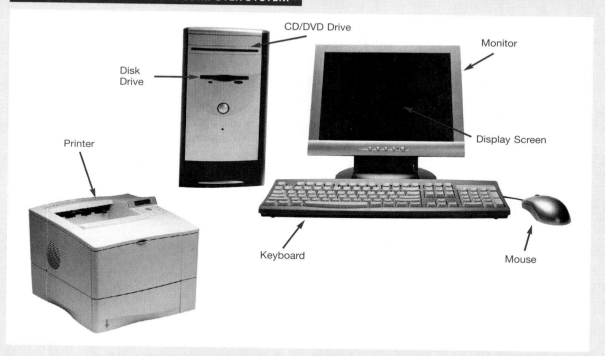

CD/DVD Drive

Monitor

Disk Drive

Display Screen

Printer

Keyboard

Mouse

B. THE COMPUTER KEYBOARD

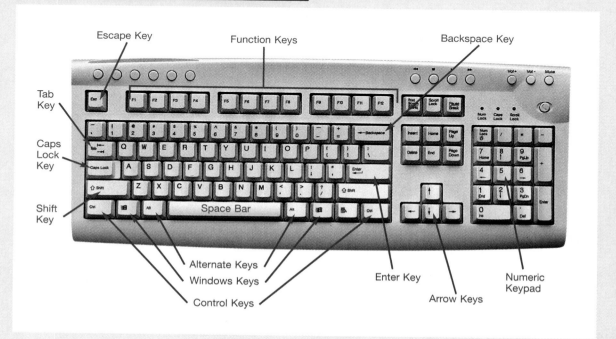

Escape Key

Function Keys

Backspace Key

Tab Key

Caps Lock Key

Shift Key

Alternate Keys

Windows Keys

Control Keys

Enter Key

Arrow Keys

Numeric Keypad

A. BUSINESS LETTER IN BLOCK STYLE

(with standard punctuation)

Date line ↓5X
September 5, 20-- ↓4X

Inside address Ms. Joan R. Hunter
Bolwater Associates
One Parklands Drive
Darien, CT 06820 ↓2X

Salutation Dear Ms. Hunter: ↓2X

Body You will soon receive the signed contract to have your organization conduct a one-day workshop for our employees on eliminating repetitive-motion injuries in the workplace. As we agreed, this workshop will apply to both our office and factory workers and you will conduct separate sessions for each group.

We revised Paragraph 4-b to require the instructor of this workshop to be a full-time employee of Bolwater Associates. In addition, we made changes to Paragraph 10-c to require our prior approval of the agenda for the workshop.

If these revisions are satisfactory, please sign and return one copy of the contract for our files. We look forward to this opportunity to enhance the health of our employees. I know that all of us will enjoy this workshop. ↓2X

Complimentary closing Sincerely, ↓4X
Writer's identification Jeffrey Olszewski
Jeffrey Olszewski, Director ↓2X

Reference initials fej

B. BUSINESS LETTER IN MODIFIED-BLOCK STYLE

(with open punctuation, multiline list, and enclosure notation)

Left tab: 3.25"
↓5X
→tab to centerpoint   May 15, 20-- ↓4X

Mr. Ichiro Xie
Bolwater Associates
One Parklands Drive
Darien, CT 06820 ↓2X

Dear Mr. Xie ↓2X

I am returning a signed contract to have your organization conduct a one-day workshop for our employees on eliminating repetitive-motion injuries in the workplace. We have made the following changes to the contract:

Multiline list 1. We revised Paragraph 4-b to require the instructor of this workshop to be a full-time employee of Bolwater Associates.

2. We made changes to Paragraph 10-c to require our prior approval of the agenda for the workshop.

If these revisions are satisfactory, please sign and return one copy of the contract for our files. We look forward to this opportunity to enhance the health of our employees. I know that all of us will enjoy this workshop. ↓2X

→tab to centerpoint   Sincerely ↓4X
Chalita Dudley
Chalita Dudley, Director ↓2X

Enclosure notation pec
Enclosure

C. BUSINESS LETTER IN SIMPLIFIED STYLE

(with single-line list, enclosure notation, and copy notation)

↓5X
October 5, 20-- ↓4X

Mr. Dale P. Griffin
Bolwater Associates
One Parklands Drive
Darien, CT 06820 ↓3X

Subject line WORKSHOP CONTRACT ↓3X

I am returning the signed contract, Mr. Griffin, to have your organization conduct a one-day workshop for our employees on eliminating repetitive-motion injuries in the workplace. We have amended the following sections of the contract:

Single-line list • Paragraph 4-b
• Table 3
• Attachment 2

If these revisions are satisfactory, please sign and return one copy of the contract for our files. We look forward to this opportunity to enhance the health of our employees. I know that all of us will enjoy this workshop. ↓4X

Rogena Kyles
ROGENA KYLES, DIRECTOR ↓2X

iww
Enclosure
Copy notation c: Legal Department

D. PERSONAL-BUSINESS LETTER IN MODIFIED-BLOCK STYLE

(with standard punctuation and international address)

Left tab: 3.25"
↓5X
→tab to centerpoint   July 15, 20-- ↓4X

Mr. Luis Fernandez
Vice President
Arvon Industries, Inc.
21 St. Claire Avenue East
International Address Toronto, ON M4T IL9
CANADA ↓2X

Dear Mr. Fernandez: ↓2X

As a former employee and present stockholder of Arvon Industries, I wish to protest the planned sale of the Consumer Products Division.

According to published reports, consumer products accounted for 19 percent of last year's corporate profits, and they are expected to account for even more this year. In addition, Dun & Bradstreet predicts that consumer products nationwide will outpace the general economy for the next five years.

I am concerned about the effect that this planned sale might have on overall corporate profits, on our cash dividends for investors, and on the economy of Melbourne, where the two consumer-products plants are located. Please ask your board of directors to reconsider this matter. ↓2X

→tab to centerpoint   Sincerely, ↓4X
Jeanine Ford
Return address Jeanine Ford
901 East Benson, Apt. 3
Fort Lauderdale, FL 33301

Reference Manual

A. BUSINESS LETTER ON EXECUTIVE STATIONERY

(7.25" x 10.5"; 1" side margins; with standard punctuation and delivery notation)

↓5X

July 18, 20--
↓4X

Mr. Rodney Eastwood
BBL Resources
52A Northern Ridge
Fayetteville, PA 17222

Dear Rodney: ↓2X

I see no reason why we should continue to consider the locality around Geraldton for our new plant. Even though the desirability of this site from an economic view is undeniable, there is not sufficient housing readily available for our workers.

In trying to control urban growth, the city has been turning down the building permits for much new housing or placing so many restrictions on foreign investment as to make it too expensive.

Please continue to seek out other areas of exploration where we might form a joint partnership.   ↓2X

Sincerely,
↓4X

Jennifer Gwatkin

Jennifer Gwatkin
Vice President for Operations   ↓2X

mme
Delivery notation By Fax

B. BUSINESS LETTER ON HALF-PAGE STATIONERY

(5.5" x 8.5"; 0.75" side margins; with standard punctuation)

↓4X

July 18, 20--
↓4X

Mr. Aristeo Olivas
BBL Resources
52A Northern Ridge
Fayetteville, PA 17222

Dear Aristeo: ↓2X

We should discontinue considering Geraldto n for our new plant. Even though the desirability of this site from an economic view is undeniable, there is insufficient housing readily available.

Please continue to search out other areas of new exploration where we might someday form a joint partnership.   ↓2X

Sincerely,
↓4X

Chimere Jones

Chimere Jones
Vice President for Operations   ↓2X

adk

C. BUSINESS LETTER FORMATTED FOR A WINDOW ENVELOPE

(with standard punctuation)

↓5X

July 18, 20--
↓3X

Ms. Reinalda Guerrero
BBL Resources
52A Northern Ridge
Fayetteville, PA 17222
↓3X

Dear Ms. Guerrero: ↓2X

I see no reason why we should even continue to consider the locality around Geraldton for our new plant. Even though the desirability of this site from an economic view is undeniable, there is insufficient housing readily available for our workers.

In trying to control urban growth, the city has been turning down the building permits for new housing or placing so many restrictions on foreign investment as to make it too expensive.

Please continue to seek out other areas of exploration where we might form a joint partnership.   ↓2X

Sincerely,
↓4X

Augustus Mays

Augustus Mays
Vice President for Operations   ↓2X

woc

D. MEMO

(with table and attachment notation)

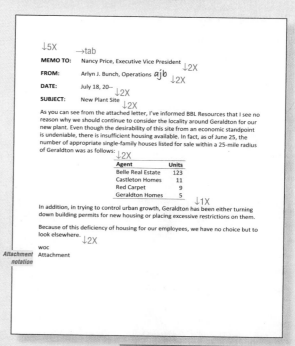

↓5X   →tab

MEMO TO: Nancy Price, Executive Vice President   ↓2X

FROM: Arlyn J. Bunch, Operations *ajb*   ↓2X

DATE: July 18, 20--   ↓2X

SUBJECT: New Plant Site   ↓2X

As you can see from the attached letter, I've informed BBL Resources that I see no reason why we should continue to consider the locality around Geraldton for our new plant. Even though the desirability of this site from an economic standpoint is undeniable, there is insufficient housing available. In fact, as of June 25, the number of appropriate single-family houses listed for sale within a 25-mile radius of Geraldton was as follows: ↓2X

Agent	Units
Belle Real Estate	123
Castleton Homes	11
Red Carpet	9
Geraldton Homes	5

↓1X

In addition, in trying to control urban growth, Geraldton has been either turning down building permits for new housing or placing excessive restrictions on them.

Because of this deficiency of housing for our employees, we have no choice but to look elsewhere.   ↓2X

woc
Attachment notation Attachment

Reference Manual

A. MULTIPAGE BUSINESS LETTER

(page 1; with standard punctuation, on-arrival notation, international address, subject line, and table)

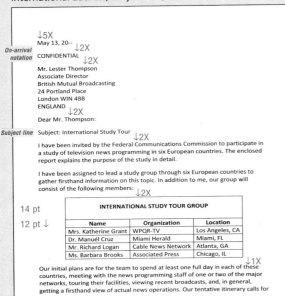

↓5X
May 13, 20-- ↓2X

On-arrival notation CONFIDENTIAL ↓2X

Mr. Lester Thompson
Associate Director
British Mutual Broadcasting
24 Portland Place
London WIN 4BB
ENGLAND ↓2X

Dear Mr. Thompson:

Subject line Subject: International Study Tour ↓2X

I have been invited by the Federal Communications Commission to participate in a study of television news programming in six European countries. The enclosed report explains the purpose of the study in detail.

I have been assigned to lead a study group through six European countries to gather firsthand information on this topic. In addition to me, our group will consist of the following members: ↓2X

14 pt

12 pt ↓

INTERNATIONAL STUDY TOUR GROUP

Name	Organization	Location
Mrs. Katherine Grant	WPQR-TV	Los Angeles, CA
Dr. Manuél Cruz	Miami Herald	Miami, FL
Mr. Richard Logan	Cable News Network	Atlanta, GA
Ms. Barbara Brooks	Associated Press	Chicago, IL

↓1X

Our initial plans are for the team to spend at least one full day in each of these countries, meeting with the news programming staff of one or two of the major networks, touring their facilities, viewing recent broadcasts, and, in general, getting a firsthand view of actual news operations. Our tentative itinerary calls for

B. MULTIPAGE BUSINESS LETTER

(page 2; with standard punctuation; multiline list; company name; and enclosure, delivery, copy, postscript, and blind copy notations)

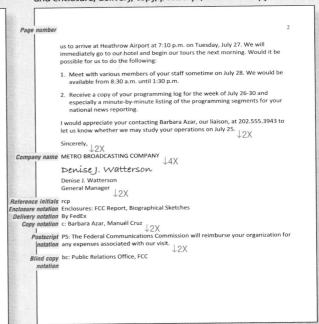

Page number 2

us to arrive at Heathrow Airport at 7:10 p.m. on Tuesday, July 27. We will immediately go to our hotel and begin our tours the next morning. Would it be possible for us to do the following:

1. Meet with various members of your staff sometime on July 28. We would be available from 8:30 a.m. until 1:30 p.m.

2. Receive a copy of your programming log for the week of July 26-30 and especially a minute-by-minute listing of the programming segments for your national news reporting.

I would appreciate your contacting Barbara Azar, our liaison, at 202.555.3943 to let us know whether we may study your operations on July 25. ↓2X

Sincerely, ↓2X

Company name METRO BROADCASTING COMPANY ↓4X

Denise J. Watterson

Denise J. Watterson
General Manager ↓2X

Reference initials rcp
Enclosure notation Enclosures: FCC Report, Biographical Sketches
Delivery notation By FedEx
Copy notation c: Barbara Azar, Manuél Cruz ↓2X
Postscript notation PS: The Federal Communications Commission will reimburse your organization for any expenses associated with our visit. ↓2X
Blind copy notation bc: Public Relations Office, FCC

C. E-MAIL MESSAGE IN MICROSOFT OUTLOOK/ INTERNET EXPLORER

D. E-MAIL MESSAGE IN MSN HOTMAIL

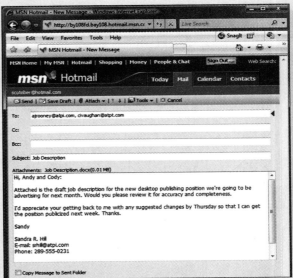

Reference Manual

A. FORMATTING ENVELOPES

A standard large (No. 10) envelope is 9.5 by 4.125 inches. A standard small (No. 6¾) envelope is 6.5 by 3.625 inches. Although either address format shown below is acceptable, the format shown for the large envelope (all caps and no punctuation) is recommended by the U.S. Postal Service for mail that will be sorted by an electronic scanning device.

Window envelopes are often used in a word processing environment because of the difficulty of aligning envelopes correctly in some printers. A window envelope requires no formatting, since the letter is formatted and folded so that the inside address is visible through the window.

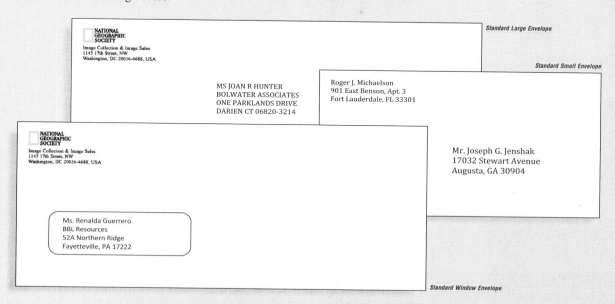

B. FOLDING LETTERS

To fold a letter for a large envelope:

1. Place the letter *face up* and fold up the bottom third.
2. Fold the top third down to 0.5 inch from the bottom edge.
3. Insert the last crease into the envelope first, with the flap facing up.

To fold a letter for a small envelope:

1. Place the letter *face up* and fold up the bottom half to 0.5 inch from the top.
2. Fold the right third over to the left.
3. Fold the left third over to 0.5 inch from the right edge.
4. Insert the last crease into the envelope first, with the flap facing up.

To fold a letter for a window envelope:

1. Place the letter *face down* with the letterhead at the top and fold the bottom third of the letter up.
2. Fold the top third down so that the address shows.
3. Insert the letter into the envelope so that the address shows through the window.

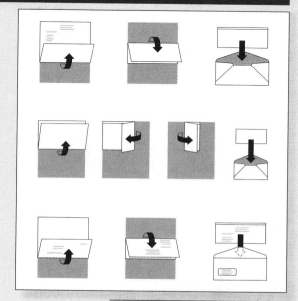

Reference Manual

A. OUTLINE

Right tab: 0.3"; left tabs: 0.4", 0.7"

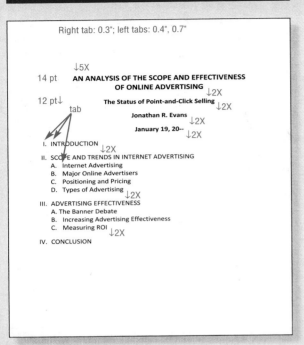

↓5X

14 pt **AN ANALYSIS OF THE SCOPE AND EFFECTIVENESS**
OF ONLINE ADVERTISING ↓2X

12 pt↓ **The Status of Point-and-Click Selling** ↓2X

tab **Jonathan R. Evans** ↓2X

January 19, 20-- ↓2X

I. INTRODUCTION ↓2X

II. SCOPE AND TRENDS IN INTERNET ADVERTISING
   A. Internet Advertising
   B. Major Online Advertisers
   C. Positioning and Pricing
   D. Types of Advertising ↓2X

III. ADVERTISING EFFECTIVENESS
   A. The Banner Debate
   B. Increasing Advertising Effectiveness
   C. Measuring ROI ↓2X

IV. CONCLUSION

B. TITLE PAGE

center page↓

14 pt **AN ANALYSIS OF THE SCOPE AND EFFECTIVENESS**
OF ONLINE ADVERTISING ↓2X

12 pt↓ **The Status of Point-and-Click Selling** ↓12X

Submitted to ↓2X

Luis Torres
General Manager
ViaWorld, International ↓12X

Prepared by ↓2X
Jonathan R. Evans
Assistant Marketing Manager
ViaWorld, International ↓2X

January 19, 20-- ↓2X

C. TRANSMITTAL MEMO

(with 2-line subject line and attachment notation)

↓5X

→ tab

MEMO TO: Luis Torres, General Manager ↓2X

FROM: Jonathan R. Evans, Assistant Marketing Manager *jre* ↓2X

DATE: January 19, 20-- ↓2X

SUBJECT: An Analysis of the Scope and Effectiveness of Current Online
Advertising ↓2X

Here is the final report analyzing the scope and effectiveness of Internet
advertising that you requested on January 5, 20--.

The report predicts that the total value of the business-to-business e-commerce
market will reach $1.3 trillion by 2003, up from $190 billion in 1999. New
technologies aimed at increasing Internet ad interactivity and the adoption of
standards for advertising response measurement and tracking will contribute to
this increase. Unfortunately, as discussed in this report, the use of "rich media"
and interactivity in Web advertising will create its own set of problems.

I enjoyed working on this assignment, Luis, and learned quite a bit from my
analysis of the situation. Please let me know if you have any questions about the
report. ↓2X

plw
Attachment

D. TABLE OF CONTENTS

Left tab: 0.5"; right dot-leader tab: 6.5"

↓5X

14 pt **CONTENTS** ↓2X ↓tab 6.5"

Reference Manual

A. BUSINESS REPORT

(page 1; with multiline list and footnotes)

Title 14 pt — ↓5X

**AN ANALYSIS OF THE SCOPE AND EFFECTIVENESS
OF ONLINE ADVERTISING** ↓2X

Subtitle 12 pt↓

The Status of Point-and-Click Selling ↓2X

Byline

Jonathan R. Evans ↓2X

Date

January 19, 20-- ↓2X

Over the past three years, the number of American households online has tripled, from an estimated 30 million in 2001 to 95 million in 2004. Juniper Online Communications predicts that by the year 2010, 120 million households, representing about 82 percent of all U.S. households, will be online. [1] ↓2X

Side head

GROWTH FACTORS ↓2X

Online business has grown in tandem with the expanding number of Internet users. Juniper predicts that the total value of business-to-business e-commerce will reach $159 billion in 2005 and is likely to reach $2.3 trillion by 2008. ↓2X

Paragraph head

Uncertainty. The uncertainties surrounding advertising on the Internet remain one of the major impediments to the expansion. All of the Internet advertising industry is today in a state of flux. ↓2X

Reasons for Not Advertising Online. A recent Association of National Online Advertisers survey found two main reasons cited for not advertising online:[2] ↓2X

1. The difficulty of determining return on investment, especially in terms of repeat business and first-time shoppers.

2. The lack of reliable tracking and measurement data.

Footnotes

[1] George Anders, "Buying Frenzy," *The Wall Street Daily,* July 12, 2006, p. R6.
[2] "eStats: Advertising Revenues and Trends in the United States," *eMarketing Home page,* August 11, 2004, <http://www.emarketing.com/estats/ad>, accessed on January 7, 2007.

B. BUSINESS REPORT

(page 3; with long quotation and table)

3

who argue that banners have a strong potential for advertising effectiveness point out that it is not the banner format itself which presents a problem to advertising effectiveness, but rather the quality of the banner and the attention to its placement. According to Mike Windsor, president of Online Interactive: ↓2X

Long quotation — indent 0.5"→

It is more a case of bad banner ads, just like there are bad TV ads. The space itself has huge potential. Unlike broadcast media, the Web offers advertisers the opportunity to reach a specific audience based on data gathered about who is surfing at a site and what their interests are.[1] ↓2X

← indent 0.5"

Thus, while some analysts continue to argue that the banner advertisement is passé, there is little evidence of its abandonment. Instead, ad agencies are focusing on increasing the banner's effectiveness. ↓2X

SCOPE AND TRENDS IN ONLINE ADVERTISING ↓2X

Starting from zero in 1994, analysts agree that the volume of Internet advertising spending has risen rapidly. However, as indicated in Table 3, analysts provide a wide range of the exact amount of such advertising. ↓2X

14 pt
12 pt ↓

TABLE 3. INTERNET ADVERTISING 2005 Estimates	
Source	Estimate
Internet Advertising Conference	$3.92 billion
Forecaster	$3.30 billion
IPC International	$3.20 billion
Brown Media	$980 million

Table source

Source: "eMarketing Research Report," *Advertising Daily,* May 3, 2006, p. 24.

The differences in estimates of total Web advertising spending is generally attributed to the different methodologies used by the research agencies to gather

[1] Lisa Napoliano, "Banner Ads Are Under the Gun—And On the Move," *The New York Financial Times,* June 17, 2005, p. D1.

C. ACADEMIC REPORT

(page 1; with indented multiline list and endnote references)

↓5SS

14 pt — **AN ANALYSIS OF THE SCOPE AND EFFECTIVENESS OF ONLINE ADVERTISING** ↓1DS

The Status of Point-and-Click Selling ↓1DS

12 pt↓

Jonathan R. Evans ↓1DS

January 19, 20- [i] ↓1DS

Over the past three years, the number of American households online has tripled, from an estimated 30 million in 2001 to more than 95 million in 2004. [i] ↓1DS

GROWTH FACTORS ↓1DS

Online business has grown in tandem with the expanding number of Internet users. Juniper predicts that the total value of business-to-business e-commerce will reach $159 billion in 2005 and will reach $2.3 trillion by 2008.

Reasons for Not Advertising Online. An Association of National Online Advertisers survey found two main reasons cited for not advertising online:[ii]

1. The difficulty of determining return on investment, especially in terms of repeat business.

2. The lack of reliable tracking and measurement data

The uncertainties surrounding advertising on the Internet remain one of the major impediments to the expansion. All of the Internet advertising industry is today in a state of flux. Some analysts argue that advertising on the Internet can

D. ACADEMIC REPORT

(last page; with long quotation and endnotes)

14

advertising effectiveness, but rather the quality of the banner and the attention to its placement. According to Mike Windsor, president of Ogilvy Interactive: [vii]

Long quotation — indent 0.5"→

It's more a case of bad banner ads, just like there are bad TV ads. The space itself has huge potential. As important as using the space within the banner creatively is to aim it effectively. Unlike broadcast media, the Web offers advertisers the opportunity to reach a specific audience based on data gathered about who is surfing at a site and what their interests are.

← indent 0.5"

From the advertiser's perspective, the most effective Internet ads do more than just deliver information to the consumer and grab the consumer's attention—they also gather information about consumers (e.g., through "cookies" and other methodologies). From the consumer's perspective, this type of interactivity may represent an intrusion and an invasion of privacy. There appears to be a shift away from the ad-supported model and toward the transaction model, wherein users pay for the content they want and the specific transactions they perform.

Endnotes

[i] Greg Anderson, "Online Buying Frenzy," *The Wall Street Financial Journal,* July 12, 2008, p. R6.
[ii] "eStats: Advertising Revenues and Expenses," *eMarketing Home page,* August 11, 2005, <http://www.emarketer.com/estats/ad>, accessed on January 7, 2007.
[iii] Bradley Jenson, Net Ratings Index Shows 14% Rise in Web Ads," *Advertising Age,* July 19, 2006, p. 18.
[iv] Tom Highland, "Web Advertising: A Decade of Growth," *Internet Advertising Conference Home page,* November 13, 2005, <http://www.iab.net/advertise>, accessed on January 8, 2007.
[v] Adrian Mandlay, "Click Here: Free Ride Doles Out Freebies to Ad Surfers," *Brand Age,* March 8, 2006, p. 30.
[vi] Andrea Peters, "High Price of Banner Ads Slips Amid Increase in Web Sites," *The Wall Street Journal,* March 2, 2007, p. B20.
[vii] Lisa Napoliano, "Banner Ads Are On the Move," *The New York Financial Times,* June 17, 2006, p. D1.

Reference Manual

A. LEFT-BOUND BUSINESS REPORT

(page 1; with endnote references and single-line list)

Left margin: 1.50" Right margin: *default* (1.00")

↓5X

14 pt **AN ANALYSIS OF THE SCOPE AND
EFFECTIVENESS OF ONLINE ADVERTISING** ↓2X

12 pt↓ **The Status of Point-and-Click Selling** ↓2X
↓2X
Aristeo Olivas ↓2X
January 19, 20-- ↓2X
↓2X

Over the past three years, the number of American households online has tripled, from an estimated 30 million in 2001 to 95 million in 2004. Juniper Online Communications predicts that by the year 2010, 120 million households, representing about 82 percent of all U.S. households, will be online.[i] ↓2X

GROWTH FACTORS ↓2X

Online business has grown in tandem with the expanding number of Internet users. Juniper online predicts that the total value of business-to-business e-commerce will reach $159 billion in 2005 and is likely to reach $2.3 trillion by 2008. ↓2X

Uncertainty. The uncertainties surrounding advertising on the Internet remain one of the major impediments to the expansion. Dating from just 1994, when the first banner ads appeared on the Hotwired home page, the Internet advertising industry is today in a state of flux. ↓2X

Some analysts argue that advertising on the Internet can and should follow the same principles as advertising on television and other visual media. Others contend that advertising on the Internet should reflect the unique characteristics of this new medium. ↓2X

Reasons for Not Advertising Online. A recent Association of National Online Advertisers survey found two reasons cited for not advertising:[ii] ↓2X

1. The difficulty of determining return on investment
2. The lack of reliable tracking and measurement data

B. BIBLIOGRAPHY

(for business or academic style using either endnotes or footnotes)

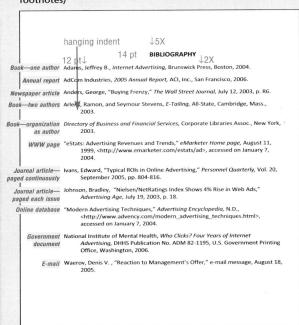

hanging indent ↓5X
12 pt↓ 14 pt **BIBLIOGRAPHY** ↓2X

Book—one author Adams, Jeffrey B., *Internet Advertising*, Brunswick Press, Boston, 2004.

Annual report AdCom Industries, *2005 Annual Report*, ACI, Inc., San Francisco, 2006.

Newspaper article Anders, George, "Buying Frenzy," *The Wall Street Journal*, July 12, 2003, p. R6.

Book—two authors Arlen, Ramon, and Seymour Stevens, *E-Tailing*, All-State, Cambridge, Mass., 2003.

Book—organization as author *Directory of Business and Financial Services*, Corporate Libraries Assoc., New York, 2003.

WWW page "eStats: Advertising Revenues and Trends," *eMarketer Home page*, August 11, 1999, <http://www.emarketer.com/estats/ad>, accessed on January 7, 2004.

Journal article— paged continuously Ivans, Edward, "Typical ROIs in Online Advertising," *Personnel Quarterly*, Vol. 20, September 2005, pp. 804-816.

Journal article— paged each issue Johnson, Bradley, "Nielsen/NetRatings Index Shows 4% Rise in Web Ads," *Advertising Age*, July 19, 2003, p. 18.

Online database "Modern Advertising Techniques," *Advertising Encyclopedia*, N.D., <http://www.advency.com/modern_advertising_techniques.html>, accessed on January 7, 2004.

Government document National Institute of Mental Health, *Who Clicks? Four Years of Internet Advertising*, DHHS Publication No. ADM 82-1195, U.S. Government Printing Office, Washington, 2006.

E-mail Waerov, Denis V. , "Reaction to Management's Offer," e-mail message, August 18, 2005.

C. MEMO REPORT

(page 1, with single-line list)

↓5X →tab

MEMO TO: Luis Torres, General Manager ↓2X

FROM: Jonathan R. Evans, Assistant Marketing Manager *jre* ↓2X

DATE: January 19, 20-- ↓2X

SUBJECT: An Analysis of the Scope and Effectiveness of Online Advertising ↓2X

Over the past three years, the number of American households online has tripled, from an estimated 30 million in 2001 to 95 million in 2004. Juniper Online Communications predicts that by the year 2010, 120 million households, representing about 82 percent of all U.S. households, will be online.[i] ↓2X

Online business has grown in tandem with the expanding number of Internet users. Juniper predicts that the total value of business-to-business e-commerce will reach $159 billion in 2005 and is likely to reach $2.3 trillion by 2008. Some experts predict an even larger volume.[ii] ↓2X

UNCERTAINTY ↓2X

The uncertainties surrounding advertising on the Internet remain one of the major impediments to the expansion. Dating from just 1994, when the first banner ads appeared on the Hotwired home page, the Internet advertising industry is today in a state of flux. Dramatic changes are frequent, and so are the repercussions of these many changes.

Some analysts argue that advertising on the Internet can and should follow the same principles as advertising on television and other visual media. Others contend that all of the advertising on the Internet should reflect the unique characteristics of this new medium.

A recent Association of National Online Advertisers survey found two main reasons cited for not advertising online:

1. The difficulty of determining return on investment
2. The lack of reliable tracking and measurement data

D. REPORTS: SPECIAL FEATURES

Margins and Spacing. Use a 2-inch top margin for the first page of each section of a report (for example, the table of contents, first page of the body, and bibliography page) and a 1-inch top margin for other pages. Use default side and bottom margins (1 inch) for all pages. If the report is going to be bound on the left, add 0.5 inch to the left margin. Single-space business reports and double-space academic reports.

Headings. Center the report title in 14-point font (press ENTER to space down before switching to 12-point font). Single-space multiline report titles in a single-spaced report and double-space multiline titles in a double-spaced report. Insert 1 blank line before and after all parts of a heading block (consisting of the title, subtitle, author, and/or date) and format all lines in bold.

Insert 1 blank line before and after side headings and format in bold, beginning at the left margin. Format paragraph headings in bold; begin at the left margin for single-spaced reports and indent for double-spaced reports. The text follows on the same line, preceded by a period and 1 space.

Citations. For business and academic reports, format citations using your word processor's footnote (or endnote) feature. For reports formatted in APA or MLA style, use the format shown on page R-10.

Reference Manual

A. REPORT IN APA STYLE

(page 1; with author/year citations)

Top, bottom, and side margins: 1"

header → Online Advertising 3

An Analysis of the Scope and Effectiveness

of Online Advertising

Jonathan R. Evans

Over the past three years, the number of American households online has

tripled, from an estimated 30 million in 2001 to 95 million in 2004. Juniper Online

Communications predicts that by the year 2010, 120 million households will be

online (Napoli, 2006).

main head → Growth Factors

Online business has grown in tandem with the expanding number of

Internet users. Juniper predicts that the total value of business-to-business e-

commerce will reach $159 billion in 2005 and is likely to reach $2.3 trillion by

2008 (Arlens & Stevens, 2005).

subhead → Uncertainty

The uncertainties surrounding advertising on the Internet remain one of

the major impediments to the expansion. Dating from just 1994, when the first

banner ads appeared on the Hotwired home page, the Internet advertising

industry is today in a state of flux.

Some analysts argue that advertising on the Internet can and should follow

the same principles as advertising on television and other visual media ("eStats,"

2007). Others contend that advertising on the Internet should reflect the unique

characteristics of this new medium.

B. REFERENCES IN APA STYLE

Top, bottom, and side margins: 1"; double-space throughout.

header → Online Advertising 14

References

hanging indent

Book—one author → Adams, J. B. (2004). *Internet advertising and the upcoming electronic upheaval.*
Boston: Brunswick Press.

Annual report → AdCom Industries. (2006). *2005 annual report.* San Francisco: ACI, Inc.

Newspaper article → Anders, G. (2003, July 12). Buying frenzy. *The Wall Street Journal,* p. R6.

Book—two authors → Arlens, R., & Stevens, S. (2003). *E-tailing.* Cambridge, MA: All-State.

Book—organization as author → *Directory of business and financial services.* (2003). New York: Corporate Libraries
Association.

WWW page → eStats: Advertising revenues and trends. (n.d.). New York: eMarketer. Retrieved
August 11, 2004, from the World Wide Web:
http://www.emarketer.com/estats/2507manu.ad

Journal article— paged continuously → Ivans, E. (2005). Typical ROIs in online advertising. *Personnel Quarterly, 20,* 804-
816.

Journal article— paged each issue → Johnson, B. (2003, July 19). Nielsen/NetRatings Index shows 4% rise in Web ads.
Advertising Age, 39, 18.

Online database → Modern advertising techniques. (1998, January). *Advertising Encyclopedia.*
Retrieved January 7, 2004, from http://www.advency.com/ads.html

Government document → National Institute of Mental Health (2006). *Who clicks? Four years of Internet
advertising* (DHHS Publication No. ADM 82-1195). Washington, DC.

C. REPORT IN MLA STYLE

(page 1; with author/page citations)

Top, bottom, and side margins: 1"
Double-space throughout.

header → Evans 1

Jonathan R. Evans

Professor Inman

Management 302

19 January 20--

An Analysis of the Scope and Effectiveness

of Online Advertising

Over the past three years, the number of American households online has

tripled, from an estimated 30 million in 2001 to 95 million in 2004. Juniper Online

Communications predicts that by the year 2010, 120 million households,

representing 62 percent of all U.S. households, will be online (Napoli D1). Online

business has grown in tandem with the expanding number of Internet users.

Juniper predicts that the total value of business-to-business e-commerce will

reach $159 billion in 2005 (Arlens & Stevens 376-379).

The uncertainties surrounding advertising on the Internet remain one of

the major impediments to the expansion. Dating from just 1994, when the first

banner ads appeared on the Hotwired home page, the Internet advertising

industry is today in a state of flux.

Some analysts argue that advertising on the Internet can and should follow

the same principles as advertising on television and other visual media ("eStats,"

D. WORKS CITED IN MLA STYLE

Top, bottom, and side margins: 1"; double-space throughout.

header → Evans 13

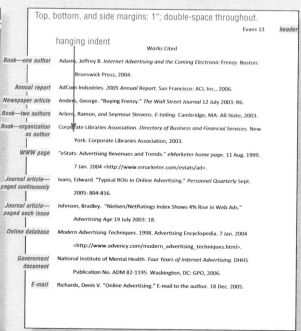

hanging indent

Works Cited

Book—one author → Adams, Jeffrey B. *Internet Advertising and the Coming Electronic Frenzy.* Boston:
Brunswick Press, 2004.

Annual report → AdCom Industries. *2005 Annual Report.* San Francisco: ACI, Inc., 2006.

Newspaper article → Anders, George. "Buying Frenzy." *The Wall Street Journal* 12 July 2003: R6.

Book—two authors → Arlens, Ramon, and Seymour Stevens. *E-tailing.* Cambridge, MA: All-State, 2003.

Book—organization as author → Corporate Libraries Association. *Directory of Business and Financial Services.* New
York: Corporate Libraries Association, 2003.

WWW page → "eStats: Advertising Revenues and Trends." *eMarketer home page.* 11 Aug. 1999.
7 Jan. 2004 <http://www.emarketer.com/estats/ad>.

Journal article— paged continuously → Ivans, Edward. "Typical ROIs in Online Advertising." *Personnel Quarterly* Sept.
2005: 804-816.

Journal article— paged each issue → Johnson, Bradley. "Nielsen/NetRatings Index Shows 4% Rise in Web Ads."
Advertising Age 19 July 2003: 18.

Online database → *Modern Advertising Techniques.* 1998. Advertising Encyclopedia. 7 Jan. 2004
<http://www.advency.com/modern_advertising_techniques.html>.

Government document → National Institute of Mental Health. *Four Years of Internet Advertising.* DHHS
Publication No. ADM 82-1195. Washington, DC: GPO, 2006.

E-mail → Richards, Denis V. "Online Advertising." E-mail to the author. 18 Dec. 2005.

Reference Manual

A. MEETING AGENDA

↓5X

14 pt **MILES HARDWARE EXECUTIVE COMMITTEE** ↓2X

12 pt↓ **Meeting Agenda** ↓2X

June 7, 20--, 3 p.m. ↓2X

1. Call to order ↓2X
2. Approval of minutes of May 5 meeting
3. Progress report on building addition and parking lot restrictions (Norman Hodges and Anthony Pascarelli)
4. May 15 draft of Five-Year Plan
5. Review of National Hardware Association annual convention
6. Employee grievance filed by Ellen Burrows (John Landstrom)
7. New expense-report forms (Anne Richards)
8. Announcements
9. Adjournment

B. MINUTES OF A MEETING

↓5X

	14 pt **RESOURCE COMMITTEE** ↓2X 12 pt↓ **Minutes of the Meeting** ↓2X **March 13, 20--** ↓1X	
ATTENDANCE	The Resource Committee met on March 13, 20--, at the Airport Sheraton in Portland, Oregon, with all members present. Michael Davis, chairperson, called the meeting to order at 2:30 p.m. ↓1X	
APPROVAL OF MINUTES	The minutes of the January 27 meeting were read and approved. ↓1X	
OLD BUSINESS	The members of the committee reviewed the sales brochure on electronic copyboards and agreed to purchase one for the conference room. Cynthia Giovanni will secure quotations from at least two suppliers. ↓1X	
NEW BUSINESS	The committee reviewed a request from the Purchasing Department for three new computers. After extensive discussion regarding the appropriate use of the computers and software to be purchased, the committee approved the request. ↓1X	
ADJOURNMENT	The meeting was adjourned at 4:45 p.m. ↓2X Respectfully submitted, ↓4X *D. S. Madsen* D. S. Madsen, Secretary	

(Note: Table shown with "View Gridlines" active.)

C. ITINERARY

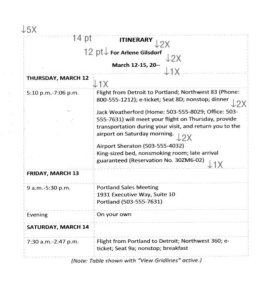

↓5X

	14 pt **ITINERARY** ↓2X 12 pt↓ **For Arlene Gilsdorf** ↓2X **March 12-15, 20--** ↓1X	
THURSDAY, MARCH 12 ↓1X		
5:10 p.m.-7:06 p.m.	Flight from Detroit to Portland; Northwest 83 (Phone: 800-555-1212); e-ticket; Seat 8D; nonstop; dinner ↓2X	
	Jack Weatherford (Home: 503-555-8029; Office: 503-555-7631) will meet your flight on Thursday, provide transportation during your visit, and return you to the airport on Saturday morning. ↓2X	
	Airport Sheraton (503-555-4032) King-sized bed, nonsmoking room; late arrival guaranteed (Reservation No. 30ZM6-02) ↓1X	
FRIDAY, MARCH 13		
9 a.m.-5:30 p.m.	Portland Sales Meeting 1931 Executive Way, Suite 10 Portland (503-555-7631)	
Evening	On your own	
SATURDAY, MARCH 14		
7:30 a.m.-2:47 p.m.	Flight from Portland to Detroit; Northwest 360; e-ticket; Seat 9a; nonstop; breakfast	

(Note: Table shown with "View Gridlines" active.)

D. LEGAL DOCUMENT

Left tabs: 1", 3.25"

12 pt↓ POWER OF ATTORNEY ↓2X

KNOW ALL MEN BY THESE PRESENTS that I, ATTORNEY LEE FERNANDEZ, of the City of Tulia, County of Swisher, State of Texas, do hereby appoint my son, Robert Fernandez, of this City, County, and State as my attorney-in-fact to act in my name, place, and stead as my agent in the management of my business operating transactions.

I give and grant unto my said attorney full power and authority to do and perform every act and thing requisite and necessary to be done in the said management as fully, to all intents and purposes, as I might or could do if personally present, with full power of revocation, hereby ratifying all that my said attorney shall lawfully do.

IN WITNESS WHEREOF, I have hereunto set my hand and seal this _____ day of _____, 20--. ↓2X

5 underscores ↑   20 underscores ↑

_____ ↓2X

SIGNED and affirmed in the presence of: ↓2X

_____ ↓2X

_____

Reference Manual

A. RESUME

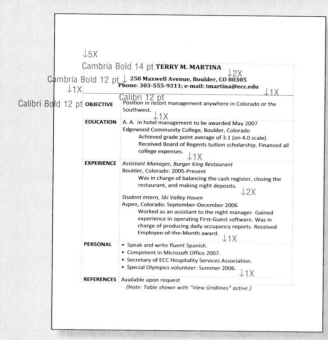

↓5X
Cambria Bold 14 pt **TERRY M. MARTINA**
↓2X
Cambria Bold 12 pt ↓ **250 Maxwell Avenue, Boulder, CO 80305**
Phone: 303-555-9311; e-mail: tmartina@ecc.edu
↓1X ↓1X

Calibri 12 pt

Calibri Bold 12 pt **OBJECTIVE**   Position in resort management anywhere in Colorado or the Southwest.
↓1X

EDUCATION   A. A. in hotel management to be awarded May 2007
Edgewood Community College, Boulder, Colorado
     Achieved grade point average of 3.1 (on 4.0 scale).
     Received Board of Regents tuition scholarship. Financed all
     college expenses.
↓1X

EXPERIENCE   *Assistant Manager, Burger King Restaurant*
Boulder, Colorado: 2005-Present
     Was in charge of balancing the cash register, closing the
     restaurant, and making night deposits.
↓2X

Student Intern, Ski Valley Haven
Aspen, Colorado: September-December 2006
     Worked as an assistant to the night manager. Gained
     experience in operating First-Guest software. Was in
     charge of producing daily occupancy reports. Received
     Employee-of-the-Month award.
↓1X

PERSONAL
- Speak and write fluent Spanish.
- Competent in Microsoft Office 2007.
- Secretary of ECC Hospitality Services Association.
- Special Olympics volunteer: Summer 2006.
↓1X

REFERENCES   Available upon request
(Note: Table shown with "View Gridlines" active.)

B. APPLICATION LETTER IN BLOCK STYLE
(with standard punctuation)

↓5X

March 1, 20-- ↓4X

Mr. Lou Mansfield, Director
Human Resources Department
Rocky Resorts International
P.O. Box 1412
Denver, CO 80214
↓2X
Dear Mr. Mansfield:
↓2X
Please consider me an applicant for the position of concierge for Suite Retreat, as advertised in last Sunday's *Denver Times*.

I will receive my A.A. degree in hotel administration from Edgewood Community College in May and will be available for full-time employment immediately. In addition to my extensive coursework in hospitality services and business, I've had experience in working for a ski lodge similar to Suite Retreats in Aspen. As a lifelong resident of Colorado and an avid skier, I would be able to provide your guests with any information they request.

After you've reviewed my enclosed resume, I would appreciate having an opportunity to discuss with you why I believe I have the right qualifications and personality to serve as your concierge. I can be reached at 303-555-9311. ↓2X

Sincerely,
↓4X
Terry M. Martina
Terry M. Martina
250 Maxwell Avenue, Apt. 8
Boulder, CO 80305
↓2X

Enclosure ↓2X

C. FORMATTING LISTS

Numbers or bullets may be used in letters, memos, and reports to call attention to items in a list. If the sequence of the items is important, use numbers rather than bullets.

❏ Begin the number or bullet at the paragraph point, that is, at the left margin for blocked paragraphs and indented 0.5 inch for indented paragraphs.
❏ Insert 1 blank line before and after the list.
❏ Within the list, use the same spacing (single or double) as is used in the rest of the document.
❏ For single-spaced documents, if all items require no more than 1 line, single-space the items in the list. If any item requires more than 1 line, single-space each item and insert 1 blank line between each item.

To format a list:

1. Type the list unformatted and press ENTER 1 time.
2. Select the items in the list (but not any blank lines).
3. Apply the number or bullet feature.
4. Decrease or increase the indent as needed to adjust the position of the list.

The three bulleted and numbered lists shown at the right are all formatted correctly.

D. EXAMPLES OF DIFFERENT TYPES OF LISTS

According to PricewaterhouseCoopers and the Internet Advertising Bureau, the following are the most common types of advertising on the Internet:

- Banner ads that feature some type of appropriate animation to attract the viewer's attention and interest.
- Sponsorship, in which an advertiser sponsors a content-based Web site.
- Interstitials, ads that flash up while a page downloads.

There is now considerable controversy about the effectiveness of banner ads. As previously noted, a central goal of banner advertisements is to increase the amount of

*****

According to PricewaterhouseCoopers, the following are the most common types of advertising on the Internet, shown in order of popularity:

1. Banner ads
2. Sponsorship
3. Interstitials

There is now considerable controversy about the effectiveness of banner ads. As previously noted, a central goal of banner advertisements is to increase the amount of

*****

According to PricewaterhouseCoopers, the following are the most common

types of advertising on the Internet:

- Banner ads that feature animation to attract the viewer's attention.
- Sponsorship, in which an advertiser sponsors a Web site.
- Interstitials, ads that flash up while a page downloads.

There is now considerable controversy about the effectiveness of banner

advertising. As previously noted, a central goal of banner advertisements is to

A. BOXED TABLE (DEFAULT STYLE)

(with subtitle, braced headings, total line, and table note)

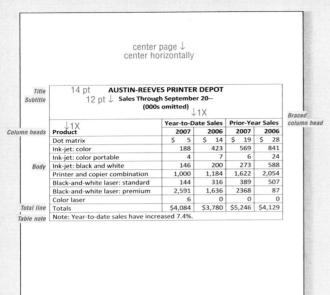

	center page ↓ center horizontally			

Title — 14 pt **AUSTIN-REEVES PRINTER DEPOT**
Subtitle — 12 pt ↓ **Sales Through September 20--**
(000s omitted)
↓1X

	Year-to-Date Sales		Prior-Year Sales	
↓1X **Product**	**2007**	**2006**	**2007**	**2006**
Dot matrix	$ 5	$ 14	$ 19	$ 28
Ink-jet: color	188	423	569	841
Ink-jet: color portable	4	7	6	24
Ink-jet: black and white	146	200	273	588
Printer and copier combination	1,000	1,184	1,622	2,054
Black-and-white laser: standard	144	316	389	507
Black-and-white laser: premium	2,591	1,636	2368	87
Color laser	6	0	0	0
Totals	$4,084	$3,780	$5,246	$4,129
Note: Year-to-date sales have increased 7.4%.				

Column heads · Body · Total line · Table note · Braced column head

B. OPEN TABLE

(with subtitle, left- and right-aligned column headings, and 2-line headings)

center page ↓
center horizontally

14 pt **SUITE RETREAT**
12 pt ↓ **New Lodging Rates**
↓1X

↓1X

Location	Rack Rate	Discount Rate	Saving
Bozeman, Montana	$ 95.75	$ 91.50	4.4%
Chicago, Illinois	159.00	139.50	12.3%
Dallas, Texas	249.50	219.00	12.2%
Las Vegas, Nevada	98.50	89.95	8.7%
Los Angeles, California	179.00	139.00	22.3%
Minneapolis, Minnesota	115.00	95.00	17.4%
New York, New York	227.50	175.00	23.1%
Orlando, Florida	105.75	98.50	6.3%
Portland, Maine	93.50	93.50	0.0%
Seattle, Washington	143.75	125.75	12.5%

C. RULED TABLE

(with table number and centered column headings)

2

an effort to reduce errors and provide increased customer support, we have recently added numerous additional telephone support services, some of which are available 24 hours a day and others available during the workday. These are shown in Table 2.
↓2X

14 pt **Table 2. WINTERLAND SKI SHOP COMPUTER AND**
TECHNICAL SUPPORT SERVICES ↓1X

12 pt↓

Support Service	Telephone	Hours
Product literature	800-555-3867	6 a.m. to 5 p.m.
Replacement parts	303-555-3388	24 hours a day
Technical documentation	408-555-3309	24 hours a day
Troubleshooting	800-555-8277	10 a.m. to 5 p.m.
Printer drivers	800-555-2377	6 a.m. to 5 p.m.
Software notes	800-555-3496	24 hours a day
Technical support	800-555-1205	24 hours a day
Hardware information	303-555-4289	6 a.m. to 5 p.m.

↓1X
We hope you will take advantage of these additional services to ensure that the computer hardware and software you purchase from Computer Supplies continues to provide you the quality and service you have come to expect from our company.

Sincerely,

Douglas Pullis

Douglas Pullis
General Manager

cds

D. TABLES: SPECIAL FEATURES

Vertical Placement. Vertically center a table that appears on a page by itself. Insert 1 blank line before and after a table appearing with other text.

Heading Block. Center and bold all lines of the heading, typing the title in all caps and 14-point font and the subtitle in upper- and lowercase and in 12-point font. If a table has a number, type the word *Table* in upper- and lowercase. Follow the table number with a period and 1 space.

Column Headings. If *all* columns in the table consist of text (such as words, phone numbers, or years), center all column headings and left-align all column entries. In all other situations, left-align all text column headings and text column entries and right-align all quantity column headings and quantity column entries. Regardless of the type of column, center braced headings. Use bold upper- and lowercase.

Column Capitalization. Capitalize only the first word and proper nouns in column entries.

Percentages and Dollars. Repeat the % sign for each number in a column (unless the heading identifies the data as percentages). Insert the $ sign only before the first amount and before a total amount. Align the $ sign with the longest amount in the column, inserting spaces after the $ sign as needed (leaving 2 spaces for each digit and 1 space for each comma).

Total Line. Add a border above a total line. Use the word *Total* or *Totals* as appropriate.

Reference Manual

A. FORMATTING BUSINESS FORMS

Many business forms can be created and filled in by using templates that are provided within commercial word processing software. Template forms can be used "as is" or they can be edited. Templates can also be used to create customized forms for any business.

When a template is opened, the form is displayed on screen. The user can then fill in the necessary information, including personalized company information. Data are entered into cells or fields, and you can move quickly from field to field with a single keystroke—usually by pressing TAB or ENTER.

B. U.S. POSTAL SERVICE ABBREVIATIONS

(for States, Territories, and Canadian Provinces)

States and Territories

Alabama	AL
Alaska	AK
Arizona	AZ
Arkansas	AR
California	CA
Colorado	CO
Connecticut	CT
Delaware	DE
District of Columbia	DC
Florida	FL
Georgia	GA
Guam	GU
Hawaii	HI
Idaho	ID
Illinois	IL
Indiana	IN
Iowa	IA
Kansas	KS
Kentucky	KY
Louisiana	LA
Maine	ME
Maryland	MD
Massachusetts	MA
Michigan	MI
Minnesota	MN
Mississippi	MS
Missouri	MO
Montana	MT
Nebraska	NE
Nevada	NV
New Hampshire	NH
New Jersey	NJ
New Mexico	NM
New York	NY
North Carolina	NC
North Dakota	ND
Ohio	OH
Oklahoma	OK
Oregon	OR
Pennsylvania	PA
Puerto Rico	PR
Rhode Island	RI
South Carolina	SC
South Dakota	SD
Tennessee	TN
Texas	TX
Utah	UT
Vermont	VT
Virgin Islands	VI
Virginia	VA
Washington	WA
West Virginia	WV
Wisconsin	WI
Wyoming	WY

Canadian Provinces

Alberta	AB
British Columbia	BC
Labrador	LB
Manitoba	MB
New Brunswick	NB
Newfoundland	NF
Northwest Territories	NT
Nova Scotia	NS
Ontario	ON
Prince Edward Island	PE
Quebec	PQ
Saskatchewan	SK
Yukon Territory	YT

C. PROOFREADERS' MARKS

Proofreaders' Marks		Draft	Final Copy
⌒	Omit space	data base	database
˅ or ˄	Insert	if hes going	if he's not going,
≡	Capitalize	Maple street	Maple Street
ℒ	Delete	a final draft	a draft
#	Insert space	allready to	all ready to
when / if	Change word	and if you	and when you
/	Use lowercase letter	our President	our president
¶	Paragraph	… to use it.¶We can	… to use it. We can
⦁⦁⦁	Don't delete	a true story	a true story
◯	Spell out	the only ①	the only one
∽	Transpose	they all see	they see all

Proofreaders' Marks		Draft	Final Copy
SS	Single-space	SS first line / second line	first line second line
ds	Double-space	ds first line / second line	first line second line
⌐	Move right	Please send	Please send
⌐	Move left	May I	May I
∿	Bold	Column Heading	**Column Heading**
ital	Italic	ital Time magazine	*Time* magazine
u/l	Underline	u/l Time magazine	Time magazine
♂	Move as shown	readers will see	readers will see

Language Arts for Business
(50 "must-know" rules)

PUNCTUATION

COMMAS

RULE 1 ▶
, direct address
(L. 21)

Use commas before and after a name used in direct address.

> Thank you, John, for responding to my e-mail so quickly.

> Ladies and gentlemen, the program has been canceled.

RULE 2 ▶
, independent clause
(L. 27)

Use a comma between independent clauses joined by a coordinate conjunction (unless both clauses are short).

> Ellen left her job with IBM, and she and her sister went to Paris.

> *But:* Ellen left her job with IBM and went to Paris with her sister.

> *But:* John drove and I navigated.

Note: An independent clause is one that can stand alone as a complete sentence. The most common coordinate conjunctions are *and, but, or,* and *nor.*

RULE 3 ▶
, introductory expression
(L. 27)

Use a comma after an introductory expression (unless it is a short prepositional phrase).

> Before we can make a decision, we must have all the facts.

> *But:* In 2004 our nation elected a new president.

Note: An introductory expression is a group of words that come before the subject and verb of the independent clause. Common prepositions are *to, in, on, of, at, by, for,* and *with.*

RULE 4 ▶
, direct quotation
(L. 41)

Use a comma before and after a direct quotation.

> James said, "I shall return," and then left.

RULE 5 ▶
, date
(L. 57)

Use a comma before and after the year in a complete date.

> We will arrive on June 2, 2006, for the conference.

> *But:* We will arrive on June 2 for the conference.

RULE 6 ▶
, place
(L. 57)

Use a comma before and after a state or country that follows a city (but not before a ZIP Code).

> Joan moved to Vancouver, British Columbia, in May.

> Send the package to Douglasville, GA 30135, by Express Mail.

> *But:* Send the package to Georgia by Express Mail.

RULE 7 ▶
, series
(L. 61)

Use a comma between each item in a series of three or more.

We need to order paper, toner, and font cartridges for the printer.

They saved their work, exited their program, and turned off their computers when they finished.

Note: Do not use a comma after the last item in a series.

RULE 8 ▶
, transitional expression
(L. 61)

Use a comma before and after a transitional expression or independent comment.

It is critical, therefore, that we finish the project on time.

Our present projections, you must admit, are inadequate.

But: You must admit our present projections are inadequate.

Note: Examples of transitional expressions and independent comments are *in addition to, therefore, however, on the other hand, as a matter of fact,* and *unfortunately.*

RULE 9 ▶
, nonessential expression
(L. 71)

Use a comma before and after a nonessential expression.

Andre, who was there, can verify the statement.

But: Anyone who was there can verify the statement.

Van's first book, *Crisis of Management,* was not discussed.

Van's book *Crisis of Management* was not discussed.

Note: A nonessential expression is a group of words that may be omitted without changing the basic meaning of the sentence. Always examine the noun or pronoun that comes before the expression to determine whether the noun needs the expression to complete its meaning. If it does, the expression is *essential* and does *not* take a comma.

RULE 10 ▶
, adjacent adjectives
(L. 71)

Use a comma between two adjacent adjectives that modify the same noun.

We need an intelligent, enthusiastic individual for this job.

But: Please order a new bulletin board for our main conference room.

Note: Do not use a comma after the second adjective. Also, do not use a comma if the first adjective modifies the combined idea of the second adjective and the noun (for example, *bulletin board* and *conference room* in the second example above).

SEMICOLONS

RULE 11 ▶
; no conjunction
(L. 97)

Use a semicolon to separate two closely related independent clauses that are *not* joined by a conjunction (such as *and, but, or,* or *nor*).

Management favored the vote; stockholders did not.

But: Management favored the vote, but stockholders did not.

RULE 12 ▶
; series
(L. 97)

Use a semicolon to separate three or more items in a series if any of the items already contain commas.

Staff meetings were held on Thursday, May 7; Monday, June 7; and Friday, June 12.

Note: Be sure to insert the semicolon *between* (not within) the items in a series.

Reference Manual

RULE 13 ▶
- number
(L. 57)

Hyphenate compound numbers between twenty-one and ninety-nine and fractions that are expressed as words.

Twenty-nine recommendations were approved by at least three-fourths of the members.

RULE 14 ▶
- compound adjective
(L. 67)

Hyphenate compound adjectives that come before a noun (unless the first word is an adverb ending in -ly).

We reviewed an up-to-date report on Wednesday.

But: The report was up to date.

But: We reviewed the highly rated report.

Note: A compound adjective is two or more words that function as a unit to describe a noun.

APOSTROPHES

RULE 15 ▶
' singular noun
(L. 37)

Use 's to form the possessive of singular nouns.

The hurricane's force caused major damage to North Carolina's coastline.

RULE 16 ▶
' plural noun
(L. 37)

Use only an apostrophe to form the possessive of plural nouns that end in *s*.

The investors' goals were outlined in the stockholders' report.

But: The investors outlined their goals in the report to the stockholders.

But: The women's and children's clothing was on sale.

RULE 17 ▶
' pronoun
(L. 37)

Use 's to form the possessive of indefinite pronouns (such as *someone's* or *anybody's*); do not use an apostrophe with personal pronouns (such as *hers, his, its, ours, theirs,* and *yours*).

She could select anybody's paper for a sample.

It's time to put the file back into its cabinet.

Reference Manual

COLONS

RULE 18 ▶
: explanatory material
(L. 91)

Use a colon to introduce explanatory material that follows an independent clause.

The computer satisfies three criteria: speed, cost, and power.

But: The computer satisfies the three criteria of speed, cost, and power.

Remember this: only one coupon is allowed per customer.

Note: An independent clause can stand alone as a complete sentence. Do not capitalize the word following the colon.

PERIODS

RULE 19 ▶
. polite request
(L. 91)

Use a period to end a sentence that is a polite request.

Will you please call me if I can be of further assistance.

Note: Consider a sentence a polite request if you expect the reader to respond by doing as you ask rather than by giving a yes-or-no answer.

QUOTATION MARKS

RULE 20 ▶
" direct quotation
(L. 41)

Use quotation marks around a direct quotation.

Harrison responded by saying, "Their decision does not affect us."

But: Harrison responded by saying that their decision does not affect us.

RULE 21 ▶
" title
(L. 41)

Use quotation marks around the title of a newspaper or magazine article, chapter in a book, report, and similar terms.

The most helpful article I found was "Multimedia for All."

ITALICS (OR UNDERLINE)

RULE 22 ▶
title or title
(L. 41)

Italicize (or underline) the titles of books, magazines, newspapers, and other complete published works.

Grisham's *The Brethren* was reviewed in a recent *USA Today* article.

Reference Manual

GRAMMAR

SENTENCES

RULE 23 ▶
fragment
(L. 21)

Avoid sentence fragments.

Not: She had always wanted to be a financial manager. But had not had the needed education.

But: She had always wanted to be a financial manager but had not had the needed education.

Note: A fragment is a part of a sentence that is incorrectly punctuated as a complete sentence. In the first example above, "but had not had the needed education" is not a complete sentence because it does not contain a subject.

RULE 24 ▶
run-on
(L. 21)

Avoid run-on sentences.

Not: Mohamed is a competent worker he has even passed the MOS exam.

Not: Mohamed is a competent worker, he has even passed the MOS exam.

But: Mohamed is a competent worker; he has even passed the MOS exam.

Or: Mohamed is a competent worker. He has even passed the MOS exam.

Note: A run-on sentence is two independent clauses that run together without any punctuation between them or with only a comma between them.

AGREEMENT

RULE 25 ▶
agreement singular
agreement plural
(L. 67)

Use singular verbs and pronouns with singular subjects; use plural verbs and pronouns with plural subjects.

I <u>was</u> happy with <u>my</u> performance.

<u>Janet and Phoenix were</u> happy with <u>their</u> performance.

Among the items discussed <u>were</u> our <u>raises and benefits</u>.

RULE 26 ▶
agreement pronoun
(L. 81)

Some pronouns (*anybody, each, either, everybody, everyone, much, neither, no one, nobody,* and *one*) are always singular and take a singular verb. Other pronouns (*all, any, more, most, none,* and *some*) may be singular or plural, depending on the noun to which they refer.

<u>Each</u> of the employees <u>has</u> finished <u>his or her</u> task.

<u>Much remains</u> to be done.

<u>Most</u> of the pie <u>was</u> eaten, but <u>most</u> of the cookies <u>were</u> left.

RULE 27 ▶
agreement intervening
words
(L. 81)

Disregard any intervening words that come between the subject and verb when establishing agreement.

The <u>box</u> containing the books and pencils <u>has</u> not been found.

<u>Alex</u>, accompanied by Tricia, <u>is</u> attending the conference and taking <u>his</u> computer.

RULE 28 ▶
agreement nearer noun
(L. 101)

If two subjects are joined by *or, either/or, neither/nor,* or *not only/but also,* make the verb agree with the subject nearer to the verb.

Neither the coach nor the <u>players are</u> at home.

Not only the coach but also the <u>referee is</u> at home.

But: <u>Both</u> the coach and the referee <u>are</u> at home.

Reference Manual

RULE 29 ▶
nominative pronoun
(L. 107)

Use nominative pronouns (such as *I, he, she, we, they,* and *who*) as subjects of a sentence or clause.

The programmer and <u>he</u> are reviewing the code.

Barb is a person <u>who</u> can do the job.

RULE 30 ▶
objective pronoun
(L. 107)

Use objective pronouns (such as *me, him, her, us, them,* and *whom*) as objects of a verb, preposition, or infinitive.

The code was reviewed by the programmer and <u>him</u>.

Barb is the type of person <u>whom</u> we can trust.

ADJECTIVES AND ADVERBS

RULE 31 ▶
adjective/adverb
(L. 101)

Use comparative adjectives and adverbs (*-er, more,* and *less*) when referring to two nouns or pronouns; use superlative adjectives and adverbs (*-est, most,* and *least*) when referring to more than two.

The <u>shorter</u> of the <u>two</u> training sessions is the <u>more</u> helpful one.

The <u>longest</u> of the <u>three</u> training sessions is the <u>least</u> helpful one.

WORD USAGE

RULE 32 ▶
accept/except
(L. 117)

***Accept* means "to agree to"; *except* means "to leave out."**

All employees <u>except</u> the maintenance staff should <u>accept</u> the agreement.

RULE 33 ▶
affect/effect
(L. 117)

***Affect* is most often used as a verb meaning "to influence"; *effect* is most often used as a noun meaning "result."**

The ruling will <u>affect</u> our domestic operations but will have no <u>effect</u> on our Asian operations.

RULE 34 ▶
farther/further
(L. 117)

***Farther* refers to distance; *further* refers to extent or degree.**

The <u>farther</u> we drove, the <u>further</u> agitated he became.

RULE 35 ▶
personal/personnel
(L. 117)

***Personal* means "private"; *personnel* means "employees."**

All <u>personnel</u> agreed not to use e-mail for <u>personal</u> business.

RULE 36 ▶
principal/principle
(L. 117)

***Principal* means "primary"; *principle* means "rule."**

The <u>principle</u> of fairness is our <u>principal</u> means of dealing with customers.

Reference Manual

MECHANICS

RULE 37 ▶
= sentence
(L. 31)

Capitalize the first word of a sentence.

Please prepare a summary of your activities.

RULE 38 ▶
= proper noun
(L. 31)

Capitalize proper nouns and adjectives derived from proper nouns.

Judy Hendrix drove to Albuquerque in her new Pontiac convertible.

Note: A proper noun is the official name of a particular person, place, or thing.

RULE 39 ▶
= time
(L. 31)

Capitalize the names of the days of the week, months, holidays, and religious days (but do not capitalize the names of the seasons).

On Thursday, November 25, we will celebrate Thanksgiving, the most popular holiday in the fall.

RULE 40 ▶
= noun #
(L. 77)

Capitalize nouns followed by a number or letter (except for the nouns *line*, *note*, *page*, *paragraph*, and *size*).

Please read Chapter 5, which begins on page 94.

RULE 41 ▶
= compass point
(L. 77)

Capitalize compass points (such as *north, south*, or *northeast*) only when they designate definite regions.

From Montana we drove south to reach the Southwest.

RULE 42 ▶
= organization
(L. 111)

Capitalize common organizational terms (such as *advertising department* and *finance committee*) only when they are the actual names of the units in the writer's own organization and when they are preceded by the word *the*.

The report from the Advertising Department is due today.

But: Our advertising department will submit its report today.

RULE 43 ▶
= course
(L. 111)

Capitalize the names of specific course titles but not the names of subjects or areas of study.

I have enrolled in Accounting 201 and will also take a marketing course.

RULE 44 ▶
general
(L. 47)

In general, spell out numbers zero through ten, and use figures for numbers above ten.

We rented two movies for tonight.

The decision was reached after 27 precincts sent in their results.

RULE 45 ▶
figure
(L. 47)

Use figures for

❑ **Dates. (Use *st*, *d*, or *th* only if the day comes before the month.)**
The tax report is due on April 15 (*not* April 15ᵗʰ)
We will drive to the camp on the 23d (or *23rd* or *23ʳᵈ*) of May.

❑ **All numbers if two or more *related* numbers both above and below ten are used in the same sentence.**
Mr. Carter sent in 7 receipts, and Ms. Cantrell sent in 22.
But: The 13 accountants owned three computers each.

❑ **Measurements (time, money, distance, weight, and percent).**
The $500 statue we delivered at 7 a.m. weighed 6 pounds.

❑ **Mixed numbers.**
Our sales are up 9½ (or *9 1/2*) percent over last year.

RULE 46 ▶
word
(L. 57)

Spell out

❑ **A number used as the first word of a sentence.**
Seventy-five people attended the conference in San Diego.

❑ **The shorter of two adjacent numbers.**
We have ordered 3 two-pound cakes and one 5-pound cake for the reception.

❑ **The words *million* and *billion* in even amounts (do not use decimals with even amounts).**
Not: A $5.00 ticket can win $28,000,000 in this month's lottery.
But: A $5 ticket can win $28 million in this month's lottery.

❑ **Fractions.**
Almost one-half of the audience responded to the question.
Note: When fractions and the numbers twenty-one through ninety-nine are spelled out, they should be hyphenated.

ABBREVIATIONS

RULE 47 ▶
abbreviate none
(L. 67)

In general business writing, do not abbreviate common words (such as *dept.* or *pkg.*), compass points, units of measure, or the names of months, days of the week, cities, or states (except in addresses).
Almost one-half of the audience indicated they were at least 5 feet 8 inches tall.
Note: Do not insert a comma between the parts of a single measurement.

RULE 48 ▶
abbreviate measure
(L. 87)

In technical writing, on forms, and in tables, abbreviate units of measure when they occur frequently. Do not use periods.

| 14 oz | 5 ft 10 in | 50 mph | 2 yrs 10 mo |

RULE 49 ▶
abbreviate lowercase
(L. 87)

In most lowercase abbreviations made up of single initials, use a period after each initial but no internal spaces.

| a.m. | p.m. | i.e. | e.g. | e.o.m. |

Exceptions: mph   mpg   wpm

RULE 50 ▶
abbreviate =
(L. 87)

In most all-capital abbreviations made up of single initials, do not use periods or internal spaces.

| OSHA | PBS | NBEA | WWW | VCR | MBA |

Exceptions: U.S.A.   A.A.   B.S.   Ph.D.   P.O.   B.C.   A.D.

Getting Started

Introduction

Microsoft® Word for Windows is a word processing program that lets you create anything from a half-page memo to a 300-page report complete with charts, tables, and artwork. Naturally, a program this powerful requires some training in order to learn how to use its many features.

The *Gregg College Keyboarding & Document Processing Manual for Microsoft Word 2007* shows you step-by-step how to perform the tasks needed to create attractive business documents. Using this manual in conjunction with your textbook will enable you to develop the keyboarding and document processing skills needed for success in the contemporary business office.

This manual will also serve as a handy, permanent reference for reviewing the features of Word that you will use most often.

FORMAT OF THIS MANUAL

The major word processing tasks are presented in the pages that follow, along with step-by-step directions for completing each task. You will be able to follow the steps easily if you remember these signals used throughout the manual:

- The computer icon (symbol) shown at the left indicates a hands-on activity that you should complete at your computer. All hands-on activities are screened in color so that you can easily identify them.
- Numbered and bulleted steps provide the exact instructions necessary to complete each task.
- When command, tab, group, button, dialog box, and other names or keyboard combinations are used in step-by-step directions, they will be shown in bold as they appear in Word **Help**. For example, "Click the **Microsoft Office Button**, and click **Save**."
- When key combinations are joined by a plus (+), press and hold down the first key while you press the second key; then release both keys. For example, "On the keyboard, press **CTRL + S**."
- Words or characters that you are to type (Agenda in the example) are shown in a different font. For example, "Center the title Agenda."

(continued on next page)

- The CD icon identifies instructions that apply only when you are using the correlated software that comes with your text. Check with your instructor or lab supervisor if you have questions.
- Those files named *practice-*.docx* are files that come with the correlated software. These files will open automatically when you start a practice exercise.
- The "Go To Textbook" icon is a reminder to return to your textbook to complete the document processing exercises for the lesson.

In addition to these signals, note the meanings of the following terms that are common to all Windows programs:

All directions in this manual apply to a right-handed mouse. If your mouse has been reset to accommodate a left-handed operator, your directions will differ.

- *Point* means to move the mouse until the mouse pointer on the screen is resting on the desired item.
- *Click* means to point to an item and then press and quickly release the left mouse button without moving the mouse.
- *Double-click* means to point to an item and then press and quickly release the left mouse button twice and without moving the mouse.
- *Drag* means to point to an item and then hold down the left mouse button while moving the mouse.
- *Right-click* means to point to an item and then press and quickly release the right mouse button.
- *Select* text means to drag across text to highlight it.

GDP DEFAULT SETTINGS

Word comes with some default settings that can change dynamically (as needed) as you use Word. In order to provide standardized, predictable settings as you work through the practice exercises and document processing jobs, GDP will automatically control certain settings. Default settings are any setting, such as margins or fonts, that are in effect automatically when Word is opened. Whenever you use Word inside of GDP to complete practice exercises and create documents, the following defaults will be preset:

1. The default **Style Set** will be changed from **Word 2007** to **Word 2003**. The **Word 2003 Style Set** will change the following defaults:

   - The default font will change from Calibri 11 to Calibri 12.

   Note: If you ever notice that the default font size inside a table is set to 11 pt rather than 12 pt, then Word's NORMAL template likely needs to be reset. To reset it, take these steps: From the **Home** tab, click the **Font Dialog Box Launcher**. From the **Font** tab, verify that the **Font** box is set to **+Body**; the **Font style** box, to **Regular**; and the **Size** box, to **12**. Click the **Default** button in the lower-left-hand corner of the window. You will see this prompt: "You are about to change the default font to (Default) +Body, 12 pt. Do you want this change to affect all new documents based on the NORMAL template?" Click **Yes**. The default font size for documents *and* tables should now be Calibri (Body) 12.

(continued on next page)

- The default line spacing will change from multiple line spacing to single line spacing.
- The default spacing after paragraphs will change from 10 pt to 0 pt.

Note: Word 2007 now uses default 1-inch margins all around. These margins will remain in effect.

2. The status bar will be changed to include the **Vertical Page Position**.
3. Some **AutoCorrect** options will be changed as follows: the first letter of sentences will *not* be automatically capitalized; double hyphens will be changed to a solid dash; and Internet and network paths will *not* be automatically changed to hyperlinks.

To change the default **Style Set** manually, refer to the callouts for the parts of a typical Word 2007 screen in Lesson 21, and then do this:

1. From the **Home** tab, in the **Styles** group, click **Change Styles**.
2. From the drop-down list, click **Style Set**, **Word 2003** (or click the desired style set).
3. From the **Home** tab, in the **Styles** group, click **Change Styles**.
4. From the drop-down list, click **Set as Default**.

To change the status bar to include the **Vertical Page Position**, do this:

1. Point to the status bar and right-click.
2. From the **Customize Status Bar** pane, click **Vertical Page Position**.

To change these **AutoCorrect** options manually, do this:

1. Click the **Microsoft Office Button**.
2. Click the **Word Options** button at the bottom of the pane.
3. From the left pane of the **Word Options** window, click **Proofing**.
4. Under **AutoCorrect options**, click the **AutoCorrect Options** button.
5. From the **AutoCorrect** tab, uncheck **Capitalize first letter of sentences**.
6. Click the **AutoFormat As You Type** tab; check **Hyphens (--) with dash (—)** and uncheck **Internet and network paths with hyperlinks**.
7. Click **OK** twice.

Note: The screen shots used throughout this manual reflect the standard Word commands that will be available to you when you use Word outside of GDP with this exception—when you access Word through GDP, you will find these additional commands available under the **Microsoft Office Button**.

- To quit Word and return to GDP, click the **Microsoft Office Button**, point to the arrow next to **GDP**, and click **Return to GDP**. If you have not saved your document, you will be prompted to save it. Click **Yes** or **No**, and you will be returned to GDP.
- To access the electronic Reference Manual, click the **Microsoft Office Button**, point to the arrow next to **GDP**, and click **Reference Manual**. See Lesson 25 for more details regarding the use of the electronic Reference Manual.

Orientation to Word Processing—A

Start Your Word Processor

To start Word from the *Gregg College Keyboarding & Document Processing* software (referred to as GDP from this point on), from the Lesson menu, click **21** to select Lesson 21 and then double-click **E. Word Processing** to begin the word processing exercise. Read any introductory screens, and click **Next** to continue. When you click **Next** on the last introductory screen, GDP will automatically launch Word and open a blank, unnamed document. You will then follow the steps in the Practice section of Lesson 21 to complete the practice exercise. Practice exercises for both Lessons 21 and 22 will begin without an **MS Word Document Options** window.

Beginning with the practice exercise in Lesson 23, you will see an **MS Word Document Options** dialog box where you can choose an option to create or edit the practice exercise or to get help or cancel the exercise if you wish to skip it. Clicking **Create** or **Edit** will launch Word automatically. If you need to revise the exercise, click **Edit . . . .** Clicking **Create . . .** will replace any existing document with either an original practice file ready for input or a blank screen depending on the exercise. Dimmed buttons indicate a choice that is unavailable at that point.

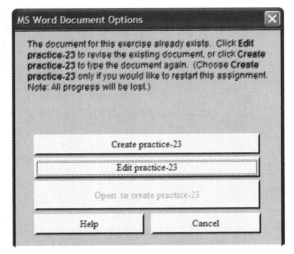

When you get to Lesson 23, practice exercises will include an MS Word Document Options dialog box before Word is launched. You will have options to create or edit a practice exercise or to get help or cancel the exercise.

When you get to Lesson 23, you will click **Create practice-23** to launch Word and then you can complete the practice exercise.

(continued on next page)

Note: If you see a GDP message that GDP cannot locate Word, check with your instructor; or if you are working at home, click **OK** and go to **Options**, **Settings**, and change your GDP settings to point to the correct path for your version of Word.

Note: To find out what version of Word you have, click the **Microsoft Office Button**, and click the **Word Options** button at the bottom of the pane. In the **Word Options** window, click **Resources**. Under **about Microsoft Word 2007**, you will see the version name and number. For more detail, click the **About** button. In the **About Microsoft Word window**, click **System Info . . .** for details about your computer specifications. Click **OK** and **Cancel** to exit.

When GDP launches Word, the Word screen might look different from a screen you might see when you launch Word outside of GDP. For example, if you start Word outside of GDP, a new blank document opens with a generic file name such as *Document1*. If you use GDP to launch Word, a document typically opens with a specific file name already assigned. GDP controls file names and other Word settings to standardize the work environment. See Getting Started, GDP Default Settings, for details.

Note: For instructions on starting Word from Windows, see Appendix A.

PRACTICE

Reminder: Complete these steps while at your computer.

1. In GDP from the **Lessons** menu, click **21**, to select Lesson 21; then double-click **E. Word Processing** to select and launch this practice exercise.
2. Read the introductory screen, follow the directions there, and click **Next**.
3. After you read the final introductory screen, click **Next**.

Note: Beginning with Lesson 23, GDP will launch practice exercises in a different way using the dialog box as shown on the previous page. You will click **Create practice-23** to begin that practice exercise.

4. In a few seconds, GDP will automatically launch Word and open a blank, unnamed document. Your screen should look similar to the one on the next page.

Note: The dynamic capabilities of Word can result in screens, toolbars, etc., that change as options are used.
Note: Depending upon your Windows settings, file extensions may or may not appear in the title bar.

(continued on next page)

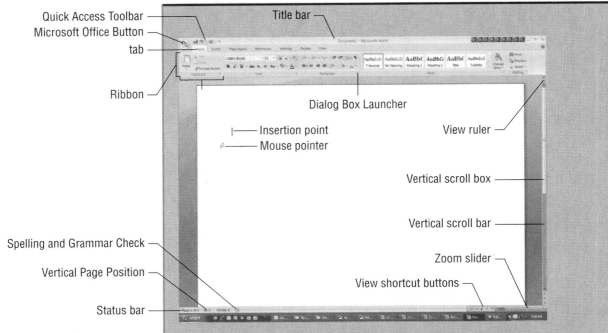

Quick Access Toolbar
Microsoft Office Button
tab
Title bar
Ribbon
Dialog Box Launcher
Insertion point
Mouse pointer
View ruler
Vertical scroll box
Vertical scroll bar
Spelling and Grammar Check
Zoom slider
Vertical Page Position
View shortcut buttons
Status bar

Reminder: To point to an item, move the mouse until the on-screen mouse pointer rests on the desired item.

5. Use your mouse to point to each item listed below on your Word screen. The mouse pointer shows the location of items on the screen. The pointer takes on different shapes, depending on the current task and on where it is positioned on the screen.

- *Title bar:* Displays the name of the current document (until documents have been saved, Word identifies them as *Document1, Document2,* and so on) and the name of the application program (*Microsoft Word*). In the illustration above, the file is named *Document2.*
- *Quick Access Toolbar:* Displays frequently used commands such as Save, Undo, and Repeat. You can add favorite commands to it.
- *Microsoft Office Button:* Displays a menu with commands to work with a file such as **New, Open, Save, Save As**, and **Print**. The right side of the menu lists recently opened documents. At the bottom are **Word Options** and **Exit Word** buttons.
- *Ribbon:* Displays seven basic tabs such as **Home, Insert**, and **Page Layout** for quick access to the popular Word commands.
- *Tab:* Displays several groups of frequently used commands related specifically to that tab such as **Clipboard, Font**, and **Paragraph** groups under the **Home** tab.
- *Group:* Displays several groups of items related specifically to that tab such as **Paste, Cut**, and **Copy** for the **Clipboard** tab.
- *Dialog Box Launcher:* Displays more options related to that group often appearing as a task pane or dialog box.

(continued on next page)

- *Insertion point:* Shows where text will appear when you type.
- *View ruler:* Displays the horizontal and vertical rulers in **Print Layout** view.
- *Vertical scroll box:* Displays different parts of a document as you drag it up or down.
- *Vertical scroll bar:* Displays different parts of a document as you click on it. Clicking the scroll bar will display one screen at a time.
- *Status bar:* Displays information about a document such as the current page, number of words in the document, and proofreading errors.
- *Vertical Page Position:* Displays the vertical page position of the insertion point from the top of the page.
- *Spelling and Grammar Check:* Displays proofreading and grammatical errors found in a document when it is clicked.
- *View Shortcuts:* Displays different document views such as **Print Layout** and **Full Screen Reading**.
- *Zoom slider:* Displays a far-away or close-up view when you drag the slider arrow or click the minus or plus signs.

Note: Keep this document open and continue reading.

Choose a Command

A command tells Word what to do. For example, you can click a command to tell Word to print a document, check your spelling, or insert a table. You can choose commands in a variety of ways such as clicking a command from the **Ribbon**, from **Mini toolbars**, or from the keyboard by using shortcut keys. An explanation of each method follows.

(continued on next page)

FROM THE RIBBON

The **Ribbon** has three basic components (tabs, groups, and commands) and seven basic tabs (**Home**, **Insert**, **Page Layout**, **References**, **Mailings**, **Review**, and **View**). When you click the desired tab, the **Ribbon** will change to display several groups of frequently used commands related specifically to that tab. For example, under the **Home** tab you will see the **Clipboard**, **Font**, **Paragraph**, **Styles**, and **Editing** groups. If your mouse has a scroll button, you can point to the **Ribbon**, roll your mouse scroll button, and move from one group to the next.

When you point to command buttons in each group and pause briefly, you will see a screen tip that displays helpful information for that feature. Take time to read this valuable information. When you click certain buttons, a command will be executed or perhaps expand to a list of related commands. Some groups include a **Dialog Box Launcher** arrow. When you click it, you will see more options related to that group often appearing as a task pane or dialog box.

Quick Access Toolbar

tab

Ribbon

group

When you point to command buttons in each group and pause briefly, you will see a screen tip that displays helpful information for that feature including any keyboard shortcuts.

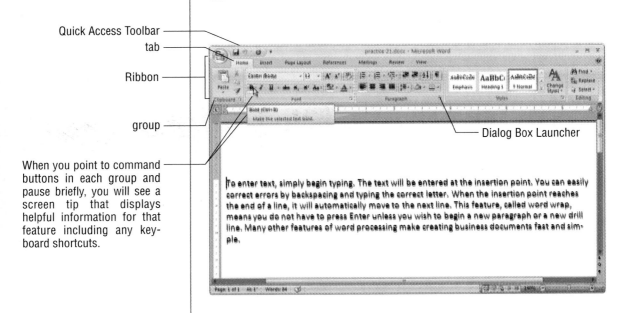

Dialog Box Launcher

(continued on next page)

Word's **Live Preview** feature allows you to quickly see how formatting options like font colors and **Quick Styles** will look in place before you actually apply the feature. When you pause over some buttons, such as the **Heading 1** button in the **Styles** group, you will see a live preview of the effect of that button in your text. By selecting text or an object and then pointing to various formatting choices, you can instantly see how a choice would appear should you select it. When you finish previewing, click the desired choice to apply it.

By selecting text (the text shown in red was selected first) and then pointing to various formatting choices, you can instantly see a "live preview" of how those choices would appear. Click the desired choice to apply it.

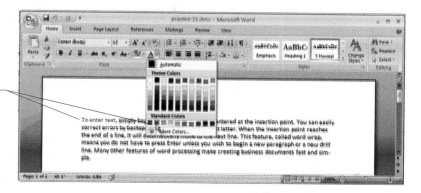

Some tabs appear only "on demand" as you are completing a certain task. For example, if you insert a picture in a document and click the picture to select it, you will see a **Picture Tools** tab appear with related groups. When you click away from the picture, the tab will disappear.

If you want to have more screen space to work on your document, you can make the groups disappear. Double-click the active tab to make the groups disappear. To make the groups reappear, double-click the active tab again.

(continued on next page)

PRACTICE *(continued)*

1. Click the **Home** tab on the **Ribbon** to make it the active tab.
2. From the **Quick Access Toolbar**, point to the **Undo** button, and note the screen tip.
3. Click the **Font Diagonal Box Launcher**.
4. Note the commands in the **Font** dialog box, and click **Cancel**.
5. Click each tab on the **Ribbon** and note the various group names.
6. Double-click the **Home** tab to make the groups disappear; double-click the **Home** tab again to make the groups reappear.

Note: Keep this document open and continue reading.

FROM THE MINI TOOLBAR

Some commands are used so frequently that Word uses **Mini toolbars** to give you quick access to those features. For example, if you select some text and point to it, you will see a faded **Mini toolbar** appear next to it. When you point to the **Mini toolbar**, it will become solid and you can click the desired command from the available options. You can also right-click the selected text to make the **Mini toolbar** appear along with a pane of frequently used commands related to the action you're performing.

PRACTICE *(continued)*

1. Type your first name, and double-click it to select it.
2. Point to the top part of the selected text, and note the faded **Mini Font** toolbar.
3. Point to the faded **Mini Font** toolbar until it becomes solid, then click away from the toolbar.

Note: Keep this document open and continue reading.

(continued on next page)

FROM THE KEYBOARD

Previous versions of Word used key combination shortcuts that started with the CTRL key such as **CTRL + C** to copy. These shortcuts and others, such as **F1** for **Help**, remain. If a button has a keyboard shortcut, the key combination will be displayed in a screen tip when you point to a button.

Word 2007 uses new shortcuts called **Key Tips** so that every button on the **Ribbon** has a shortcut and no memorizing is required. Press ALT to make the **Key Tip** badges appear for each tab on the **Ribbon**, the **Quick Access Toolbar**, and the **Microsoft Office Button**. When you press ALT, you move into command mode out of text entry mode. Then, when you press the desired **Key Tip** badge letter on the keyboard, all the **Key Tips** for the commands under that tab appear.

Note: If you press the wrong **Key Tip** badge letter, press ESC to back up one layer.

When the **Key Tips** are displayed, you can use the arrow keys on the keyboard to move around the **Ribbon** left or right through the tabs or from the **Home** or **Insert** tab, up to the **Quick Access Toolbar** and **Microsoft Office Button**. The **Key Tips** will disappear but you can get them back by pressing ALT twice. When the desired command is in view, press ENTER to activate it. You can also use the TAB key and SHIFT + TAB to cycle through commands.

PRACTICE *(continued)*

1. If necessary, click the **Home** tab on the **Ribbon** to make it the active tab.
2. From the **Font** group, point to the **Bold** button and note the screen tips and the key combination shortcut **CTRL + B**.
3. If necessary, double-click your name to select it again.
4. Press ALT to make the **Key Tip** badges appear; then press **H** on the keyboard to make the **Key Tip** badges appear in the groups under the **Home** tab.

Note: You may have to wait a few seconds for the **Key Tips** to appear.

5. Press **1** on the keyboard to bold your name.
6. Press ALT to make the **Key Tip** badges appear, then press the up arrow on the keyboard to move up to the **Quick Access Toolbar** from the **Home** and **Insert** tabs or press the left and right arrows to move around the tabs.
7. Press ALT to make the **Key Tip** badges appear, then press the TAB key and SHIFT + TAB to cycle through commands.

Note: Keep this document open and continue reading.

(continued on next page)

FROM THE QUICK ACCESS TOOLBAR

The **Quick Access Toolbar** is located to the right of the **Microsoft Office Button** and displays frequently used commands such as **Save, Undo**, and **Repeat**. You can add favorite commands to it by clicking the list arrow to the right of the toolbar and clicking the desired choice.

PRACTICE *(continued)*

1. If necessary, click the **Home** tab on the **Ribbon** to make it the active tab.
2. From the **Quick Access Toolbar**, click the **Undo** button repeatedly until you return to a blank screen.

Note: Keep this document open and continue reading.

Open a File

When you use GDP to start Word to complete a practice exercise, either a blank document or a document with text already entered will open automatically, ready for your input. After Word has started, you might need to open a document that is saved on a floppy disk, a removable disk, or the hard drive. There are several ways to open a saved file.

To open a file:

Open button

1. Click the **Microsoft Office Button**, and click the **Open** button.
   Or: On the keyboard, press CTRL + O.

   Note: When you click the **Microsoft Office Button**, the names of recently opened documents appear on the right under the **Recent Documents**. To open one of the recent documents, click the desired document name. To keep a file in the **Recent Documents** list, click the **Pin this document to the Recent Documents list** button to the right of the document name. When a document is pinned to the **Recent Documents** list, the pin button looks like a push pin viewed from the top.

(continued on next page)

2. From the **Open** dialog box, click the list arrow in the **Look in** box to see a drop-down list of other folders.

When the desired file is listed, double-click that file name to open the file.

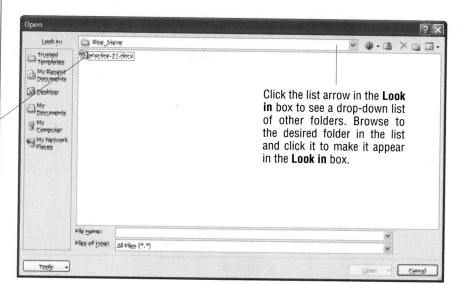

Click the list arrow in the **Look in** box to see a drop-down list of other folders. Browse to the desired folder in the list and click it to make it appear in the **Look in** box.

Note: Your dialog box will differ depending on your computer and whether you are working from the Home or Network installation of GDP.

Note: Depending upon your Windows settings, file extensions may or may not appear.

3. Browse to the desired folder in the list and click it to make it appear in the **Look in** box.

4. When the desired file is listed under the **Name** column, double-click that file name to open the file.

Note: If the list of files is too long to display all at once, you may have to scroll though the list until the desired file is visible.

(continued on next page)

PRACTICE *(continued)*

Note: In this practice exercise, you will manually open the file named *practice-21* to learn how to open a file manually. Automatic opening of files will begin with the practice exercise in Lesson 23.

1. Open the file named *practice-21*. Note the following document is displayed on your screen.

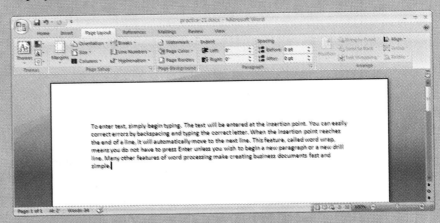

2. Note that the title bar now displays the file name *practice-21*.

Note: Keep this document open and continue reading below.

Quit Your Word Processor

To quit Word and return to GDP:

1. Click the **Microsoft Office Button**, point to the arrow next to **GDP**, and click **Return to GDP**.
2. If you have not saved your document, you will be prompted to save it. Click **Yes** or **No**, and you will be returned to GDP.

Note: If you're not using GDP, see the instructions for quitting Microsoft Word in Appendix A.

(continued on next page)

PRACTICE *(continued)*

1. Quit Word and return to GDP.

Note: If you are prompted to save changes, click **No**.

Note: You should always quit Word by clicking the **Microsoft Office Button** and then clicking **GDP, Return to GDP**, to ensure that your files are properly saved. Do *not* click the **Microsoft Office Button**, followed by the **Close** button or you might lose your work. From this point forward, "return to GDP" will be used to mean quit Word and return to GDP.

Note: If you need to return to this practice exercise later to repeat it, click **Next** to move through the introductory screens in GDP and then start again with step 1 on page 5.

Orientation to Word Processing—B

Navigate in a File

Do not confuse the insertion point with the mouse pointer (the mouse pointer is typically either an arrow or I-shaped symbol that shows the location of the mouse on the screen).

The insertion point (a blinking vertical bar) shows where text will appear in the document as you type. If you want to insert text in another part of the document, you must first move the insertion point.

To move the insertion point to a different position in your document, do one of the following:

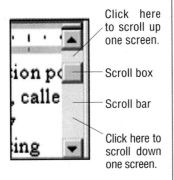

Click here to scroll up one screen.

Scroll box

Scroll bar

Click here to scroll down one screen.

To Navigate:	With the Mouse:	On the Keyboard:
Anywhere	Click where you want to position the insertion point.	Use the arrow keys to move to where you want to position the insertion point.
Through the document	Click the scroll bar (the area above or below the scroll box) to display the previous screen or to display the next screen.	Press **PAGE UP** to move backward through the document one screen at a time or **PAGE DOWN** to move forward through the document one screen at a time.
To the beginning or end of the line	Click at the beginning or end of the line.	Press **HOME** to move to the beginning of the line or **END** to move to the end of the line.
To the beginning or end of the document	Drag the scroll box to the top or bottom of the vertical scroll bar.	Press **CTRL+HOME** to move to the beginning of the document or **CTRL+END** to move to the end of the document.

Note: Using the scroll bar or scroll box does **not** move the insertion point. After navigating through text using the scroll bar or box, click in the text to move the insertion point.

(continued on next page)

PRACTICE

Note: You will manually open the file named *practice-22* in this exercise to practice what you learned in Lesson 21. Beginning with Lesson 23, GDP will launch practice exercises in a different way using the dialog box as shown on page 4. You will click **Create practice-23** to begin that practice exercise.

1. From the **Lessons** menu in GDP, click **22**, to select Lesson 22; then double-click **E. Word Processing**.
2. Read the introductory screen, follow the directions there, and click **Next**.
3. After you read the final introductory screen, click **Next**.
4. Open the file named *practice-22*.

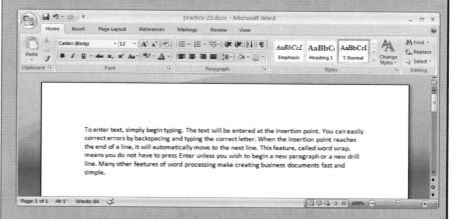

5. Locate the mouse pointer and the insertion point on the screen above and on your own computer screen.
6. Move the insertion point to the end of the document.
7. Move the insertion point immediately to the left of the "T" in "This" in line 3. What would happen if you pressed **BACKSPACE** now? What would happen if you pressed **DELETE**?
8. Move to the beginning of the same line (line 3).
9. Move to the beginning of the document.

Note: Keep this document open and continue reading.

(continued on next page)

Save a File

When you create a document, Word temporarily stores it in the computer's memory and assigns it a temporary name. To save a document permanently (so that you can open it and work on it again), you must save it on a floppy disk, a removable disk, or the hard drive. You don't have to wait until you finish a document to save it. To avoid accidental loss of data, save your work frequently.

To save a file for the first time:

1. Click the **Microsoft Office Button**, and click **Save**.

   Or: From the **Quick Access Toolbar**, click **Save**.
   Or: On the keyboard, press **CTRL + S**.

2. After the **Save As** window appears, click the list arrow in the **Save in** box to browse to the desired folder.
3. Click the list arrow in the **Save as type** box, and click **Word Document (*.docx)**. Word automatically adds the selected extension *.docx* to your file name.

   Note: The display of file extensions is controlled by Windows. Depending on your system setup, you may or may not see file extensions.

4. Type the desired file name in the **File name** box, and click **Save**.

   Note: Depending upon your Windows settings, file extensions may or may not appear.

If necessary, browse to the drive where you want to save the document.

If necessary, type a new name for the document.

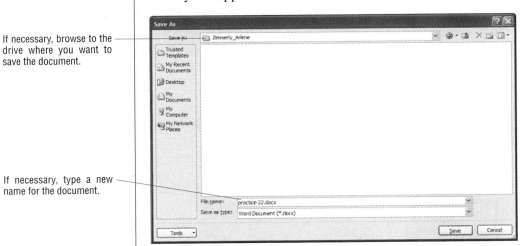

Word assigns a temporary file name to each document you create, consisting of the first few words in the document. This temporary name is selected (highlighted). Type your preferred file name; the temporary name will be erased.

(continued on next page)

When you start Word from GDP in order to type a document processing job in the textbook, a blank, named document will open automatically, ready for your input. When you use the **Save** command, you will **not** need to type a file name since the file was already assigned a specific name and will be saved with the same name. However, in this practice exercise, you will manually type a file name so that you can practice using the **Save** and **Save As** features.

Note that the file name has been changed to *student-22.docx.* Depending upon your Windows settings, the file extension *docx* may not appear in the title bar.

A file name can include upper- and/or lowercase letters, numbers, spaces, and a few common symbols such as the hyphen or underline. In general, shorter file names are preferred because they are easier to display in Windows' dialog boxes.

To save an existing document:

1. Click the **Microsoft Office Button**, and click **Save**.

> **Or:** On from the **Quick Access Toolbar**, click **Save**.
> **Or:** On the keyboard, press **CTRL + S**.

Note: If you wish to save an existing file under a different name or if you want to keep the original version of a file and then make changes to the newly saved file, click the **Microsoft Office Button**, and click **Save As**. In the **Save As** window, in the **File name** box, the existing document name will be highlighted. Browse to a new location if desired, type the new file name, and click **Save**.

PRACTICE *(continued)*

1. Move to the end of the document, and press **ENTER** 2 times.
2. Type your first and last name.
3. Click the **Microsoft Office Button**, and click the **Save As** button.
4. Save this file with the new file name *student-22*, and click **Save**. Depending upon your Windows settings, file extensions may or may not appear in the title bar. Your screen should now look like this.

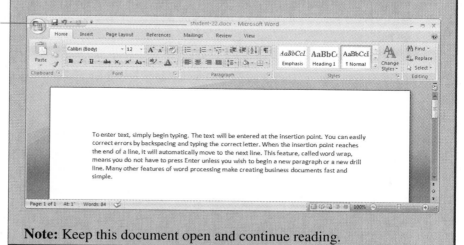

Note: Keep this document open and continue reading.

(continued on next page)

Close a File

Close button

1. Click the **Microsoft Office Button**, and click **Close**.

   Or: On the keyboard, press **CTRL + W**.
   Or: Click the **Close** button in the upper-right-hand corner of the document window.

   If it's a new document or an existing document to which you made changes, a dialog box appears asking if you want to save the document. To save your document or to save any changes, click **Yes**. If more than one document is open, a dialog box will appear for each document. Choose **Yes** to save the document or any changes.

PRACTICE *(continued)*

1. Move the insertion point to the top of the document and type today's date. Use the backspace key to correct any errors.
2. Press **ENTER** 2 times to insert 1 blank line after the date.
3. Close the document. When prompted to save changes, click **No**.

New

When you start Word outside of GDP, a new blank document (named *Document1* or *Document2,* etc.) appears on the screen, ready for you to begin typing. When you finish and close that document using the **Close** button, Word will also close unless there is an additional Word document open. If you want to close the Word file but keep Word open, do this: click the **Microsoft Office Button**, and click **Close** or on the keyboard, press **CTRL + F4**.

You cannot type in the blank window that appears when you close an open document.

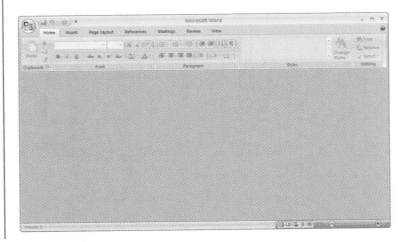

(continued on next page)

New button

To continue working, you must either open an existing document or create a new document.

To create a new document:

1. On the keyboard, press **CTRL + N**.

Or: Click the **Microsoft Office Button**, and click **New**. In the **New Document** window, under **Blank and recent**, double-click the **Blank document** button.

Note: It is not necessary to close one document before opening another one. You can have several documents open at the same time and switch back and forth among them by clicking the **View** tab and one of the following buttons: **Arrange All** to tile all open windows side by side or **Switch Windows** to switch to a currently open window from the drop-down list. You can also press **CTRL + F6** on the keyboard or click the document button on the Windows status bar if it is available depending upon your Windows setup.

PRACTICE *(continued)*

 Textbook

1. Create a new document and type your name.
2. Open the file named *practice-22*.
3. Click the **View** tab and switch to the document with your typed name using one of the following buttons: **Arrange All** to tile all open windows side by side or **Switch Windows** to switch to a currently open window from the drop-down list.
4. To return each window to normal size, switch windows and click the **Maximize** button in the upper-right-hand corner of each window.
5. Close the new file without saving it (as well as any other open files) and return to GDP.

Orientation to Word Processing—C

Select Text

To modify existing text, you must first select the text you want to change. You can then make any changes you wish; for example, you might want to change the selected text to italic or delete the text. Text that you select is highlighted—that is, the characters appear with a dark background and light letters, as shown in the following illustration:

The pointer is positioned in the **Selection bar,** the area immediately to the left of the text.

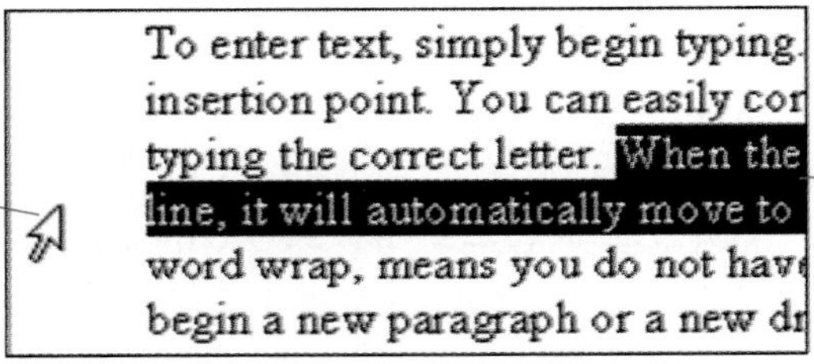

To enter text, simply begin typing. insertion point. You can easily cor typing the correct letter. When the line, it will automatically move to word wrap, means you do not have begin a new paragraph or a new dr

Selected text is highlighted.

To select (highlight) text using the mouse, do one of the following:

When you double-click to select a word, Word also selects the space after the word.

To Select:	Do This:
Any amount of text	Point and drag over the text you want to select.
A word	Double-click the word.
A line	Click in the **Selection bar** to the left of the line.
A sentence	Hold down **CTRL** and click anywhere in the sentence.
A paragraph	Double-click in the **Selection bar** next to the paragraph (*or* triple-click anywhere in the paragraph).
The entire document	Triple-click anywhere in the **Selection bar** (*or* press **CTRL+A**).

Note: To select any amount of text using the keyboard, first position the insertion point at the beginning of the text you want to select. Then hold down **SHIFT** and press the right and/or down arrow keys to extend the selection or click at the end of the selection.

If you accidentally select text, *deselect* the text (that is, cancel the operation) by clicking anywhere on the screen or by pressing any arrow key.

(continued on next page)

PRACTICE

Note: The file named *practice-23* has been opened for you automatically. From this point forward, practice exercise files will be opened automatically when Word is launched. The document below should be displayed on your screen, ready for your input. The first step in your practice exercises assumes that the practice document is already open and ready for input.

Selection bar area ——

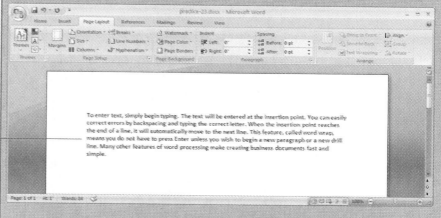

1. Move the insertion point to the beginning of the document.
2. Press **TAB** to indent the first line of the paragraph. Note that the words "can easily" move to the second line.

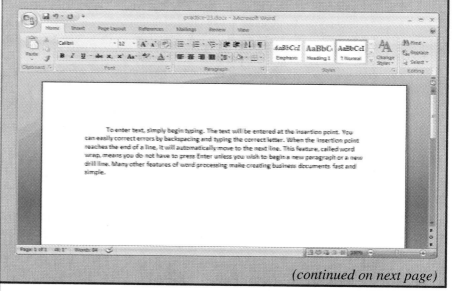

(continued on next page)

3. Select the word "automatically" in the third line by double-clicking anywhere in the word; then delete the word by pressing **BACKSPACE**.
4. Move the insertion point immediately to the left of "T" in "This" in line 3. Delete the space to the left by pressing **BACKSPACE**; then start a new paragraph at this point by pressing **ENTER** (to begin a new line). Press **TAB** to indent the line.
5. Select the second paragraph by double-clicking the **Selection bar** area next to the paragraph or by triple-clicking anywhere in the paragraph.
6. Select the entire document by pressing **CTRL + A**. Now deselect the document by clicking anywhere on the screen or by pressing any arrow key. (When you press an arrow key, the text is no longer highlighted and the insertion point moves to the beginning or end of the document.)
7. Select the words "word processing" in the last sentence. In their place, type the words `Microsoft Word for Windows`. Your screen should now look like the following illustration:

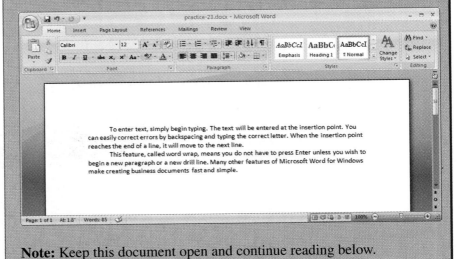

Note: Keep this document open and continue reading below.

Bold

One way of making parts of a document (such as a report title) stand out is to format the text in bold. You can either bold text as you type or bold existing text.

To bold text as you type:

(continued on next page)

Bold button

This is bold text.

This is not bold.

1. From the **Home** tab, **Font** group, click the **Bold** button.

   Or: On the keyboard, press **CTRL + B**.

2. Type the text you want to appear in bold.
3. Click the **Bold** button or press **CTRL + B** again to turn off bold, and note that the text appears in bold on the screen.

   To bold existing text:

1. Select the text you want to appear in bold.
2. Click the **Bold** button or press **CTRL + B**.

Note: The **Bold** command is a "toggle" command. Giving the command once turns **Bold** on; giving the command twice in succession turns it on and then off.

   To remove bold formatting:

1. Select the text.
2. Click the **Bold** button or press **CTRL + B** again.

PRACTICE *(continued)*

1. Move to the end of the first paragraph. Space 1 time after the period, turn on bold, type `Amazing!`, and then turn off bold.
2. Select the words "word wrap" in line 4 and then bold them.
3. Remove the bold formatting from the word "`Amazing!`" in line 3.
4. In the last sentence, select and then bold "`Microsoft Word for Windows.`"

   Your screen should now look like this:

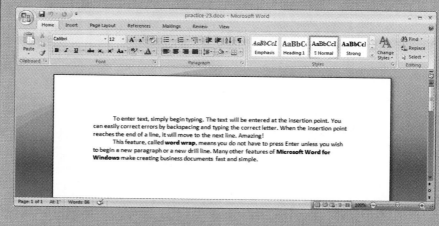

Note: Keep this document open and continue reading on the next page.

(continued on next page)

Undo/Redo a Command

To cancel a command before it has been executed or to deselect text, press **Esc**, click elsewhere on the screen, or press any arrow key. Once a command has been executed and you realize you made a mistake, you can usually reverse the last several actions.

UNDO A COMMAND

Undo button

To undo a command:

1. From the **Quick Access Toolbar**, click the **Undo** button.

Or: On the keyboard, press **CTRL + Z**.

If you want to undo an action other than the most recent one, click the arrow to the right of the **Undo** button. Clicking the arrow will display a list of actions with the most recent action at the top. Select and click the actions you want to undo. Clicking an action anywhere below the first one undoes all actions up to and including that selected action.

REDO A COMMAND

Redo button

To redo a command:

1. From the **Quick Access Toolbar**, click the **Redo** button.

Or: On the keyboard, press **CTRL + Y**.

Repeat button

Note: The **Redo** button is not always available. The button dynamically changes between **Redo** and **Repeat**. Immediately after you have used **Undo**, the **Redo** button will appear.

PRACTICE *(continued)*

1. Move the insertion point to the end of the document (after the word "simple.").
2. Press **ENTER** to begin a new paragraph.
3. Press **Tab**. Type this sentence: `Word processing makes sense (and cents) in the contemporary office.`
4. Use the **Undo** command to undo (erase) the sentence you just typed.
5. Use the **Redo** command to reinsert the sentence. Your screen should now look like this:

(continued on next page)

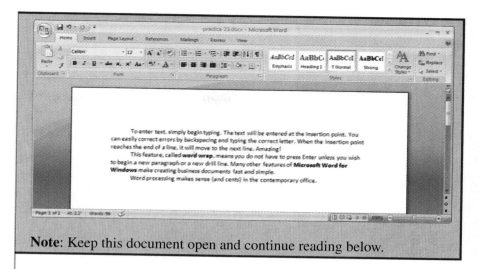

Note: Keep this document open and continue reading below.

Help

Word's extensive online Help contains all the information you need to use Word. Help is available in many places throughout the program and in a variety of formats.

To open the **Word Help** home page:

Microsoft Word Help button

1. Click the **Microsoft Office Word Help** button in the upper-right-hand corner of the Word window.

Or: On the keyboard, press **F1**.

Note: You might have to press the **Help** button a second time to open the **Word Help** home page.

(continued on next page)

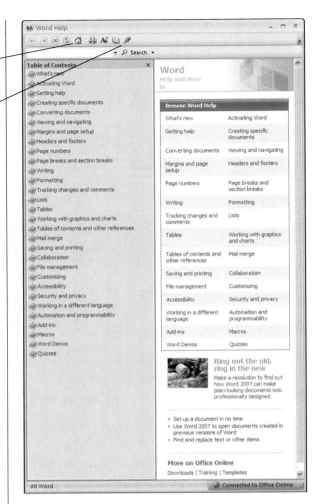

Home
button

Not on Top
button (toggles to
Keep on Top)

Show Table of Contents
button

2. Type any keywords in the search box and click the **Search** button.
3. In the **Table of Contents** pane, scroll down and click the **Word Demos** link for some excellent demonstrations of Word.

   Note: If the **Table of Contents** pane is not displayed, click the **Show Table of Contents** button. This button toggles between **Show Table of Contents** and **Hide Table of Contents**.

4. In the **Table of Contents** pane, click the **Getting Help** link for some excellent Word resources such as these links: **Interactive: Word 2003 to Word 2007 command reference guide** and **Find answers from other users in the Word community** (particularly **Word Discussion Groups**).
5. Click the **Home** button anytime to return to the **Word Help** home page, scroll to the bottom of the screen on the right pane under the **More on Office Online**, and click the **Training** link for self-paced training courses at the Microsoft Office Online Web site.

(continued on next page)

Note: Click the **Not On Top** button to pin the **Help** window so it always displays on top of all Word windows. The button name toggles to **Keep On Top**. Click it again to unpin the **Help** window.

Note: The first time you use the **Help** feature in Microsoft Office programs, the **Help** window appears in a default location and size on your screen. You can change the size and position of the **Help** window. When you later reopen the **Help** window, the settings that you made previously are maintained.

To get help on a particular command:

1. Point to a command on the **Ribbon**, and read the screen tip for more information.
2. If you see the message "Press F1 for more help." at the bottom of the screen tip, continue to rest the pointer on the command and press **F1** to get more information.

Note: Reading screen tips and pressing **F1** when you see it displayed in a screen tip is by far the easiest way to get context-sensitive help.

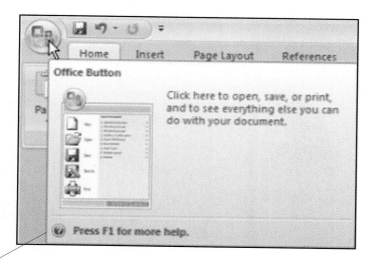

When you see this message, continue to rest the pointer on the command and press **F1** to get more information.

To get context-sensitive help while in a dialog box:

1. Click the **Microsoft Office Word Help** button in the upper-right-hand corner of the Word window.

   Or: On the keyboard, press **F1**.

(continued on next page)

When you see the **Microsoft Office Word Help** button in the upper-right-hand corner of a dialog box, click it or press **F1** on the keyboard to get context-sensitive help on the features in that dialog box.

PRACTICE *(continued)*

1. Click the **Microsoft Office Word Help** button in the upper-right-hand corner of the Word window.
2. Type "bold" in the **Search** box and click the **Search** button.
3. In the **Searched for** list, click any related link and read the information. Note that in the **Table of Contents** pane, you will see the list expand to display a link to related information.
4. In the **Table of Contents** pane, scroll down and click the **Word Demos** link.
5. Click any demo link and explore it.
6. Click the **Home** button to return to the Word Help home page; scroll to the bottom of the screen on the right pane under the **More on Office Online**.
7. If you have an Internet connection, click the **Training** link for self-paced training courses at the Microsoft Office Online Web site. If not, skip this step.
8. Point to the **Microsoft Office Button**, read the screen tip, continue to rest the pointer on the command, and press **F1** to get more information on this button.
9. From the **Home** tab, click the **Dialog Box Launcher** arrow on the **Font** group; click the **Help** button, and read any related information.
10. Save the changes to *practice-23* and return to GDP.

Go To Textbook

Orientation to Word Processing—D

Preview Pages Before Printing

Use **Print Preview** to see how your document will look when printed. To preview a document before printing:

1. Click the **Microsoft Office Button**, point to the arrow next to **Print**, and then click **Print Preview**.

   Or: On the keyboard, press CTRL + F2.

   Your formatted document appears as a full page in the window, and a **Print Preview** tab appears with groups below it.

2. Move the mouse pointer over the document. The pointer turns into a magnifying glass icon. Click anywhere in the document to view a magnified portion of the document; click again to return to the original magnification.

3. From the **Preview** group, uncheck **Magnifier** to change the mouse pointer back to its normal status. You can now edit the document.

4. Click the **Close Print Preview** button to close the window or press **Esc** on the keyboard to return to editing mode.

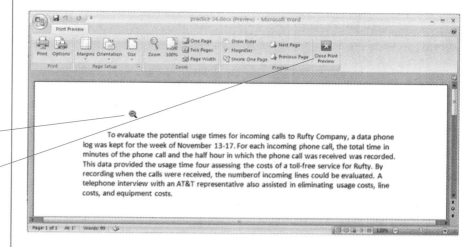

Magnifier icon

Close Print Preview button

(continued on next page)

PRACTICE

1. Click the **Microsoft Office Button**, point to the arrow next to **Print**, and then click **Print Preview**.
Your screen should look similar to this:

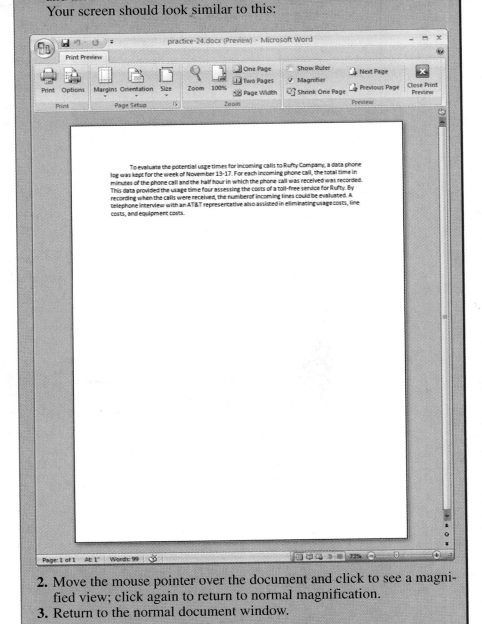

2. Move the mouse pointer over the document and click to see a magnified view; click again to return to normal magnification.

3. Return to the normal document window.

Note: Keep this document open and continue reading.

(continued on next page)

Check Spelling and Grammar

Spelling and Grammar Check
button when errors are present

Spelling and Grammar Check
button when no errors are present

Word's spelling and grammar tool checks your document for spelling, grammar, and typographical errors. When automatic spelling and grammar checking is active, spelling and grammar are checked as you type. Word marks possible spelling errors with a red wavy line and possible grammar errors with a green wavy line.

To correct a spelling error immediately, right-click the word marked with the red wavy line to display a list of suggested spellings or corrections; then click the desired choice, such as **Ignore, Ignore All**, or **Add to Dictionary**. To correct a grammar error immediately, right-click the word marked with a green wavy line; click **Grammar**, and click the desired choice such as **Ignore Once** or **Cancel** if the choices don't apply. For more detailed information, click **About This Sentence**.

To manually check spelling and grammar:

1. From the **Review** tab, **Proofing** group, click the **Spelling & Grammar** button.

   Or: On the keyboard, press **F7**.
   Or: On the status bar, click the **Spelling and Grammar Check** button when errors are present. Word will move to each error one by one and display the same choices as when you right-click the word.

   Word scrolls through the document. If the program finds a problem, it displays the **Spelling and Grammar** dialog box.

(continued on next page)

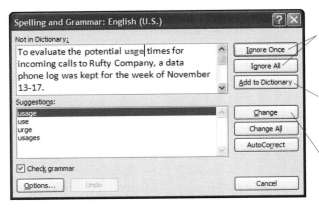

Click **Ignore Once** or **Ignore All** if the word is spelled correctly.

Click **Add to Dictionary** to add the word to Word's custom dictionary so the word will not be marked again.

Click **Change** to accept the highlighted word in the **Suggestions** box.

2. Each time the program stops for a spelling error, do one of the following:
   - If a word in the **Suggestions** list is the correct spelling, select that word, and then click **Change**.
   - If the word in the **Not in Dictionary** box is spelled correctly, click **Ignore Once** (or **Ignore All** if you want the speller to ignore all occurrences of this word in your document).

   Note: If you want to add this word to the custom dictionary so that it will not be marked again, click **Add to Dictionary**.

   - If the correct word is not displayed in the **Suggestions** list, click on the highlighted word in the **Not in Dictionary** box, type the correction, then click **Change**.

3. Each time the program stops for a grammar error, do one of the following:
   - Compare the description of the error with the suggested correction in the **Suggestions** box.
   - If the change is appropriate, click **Change**.
   - If the change is not appropriate, click **Ignore Once** or **Ignore All**.

4. When the dialog box appears with the message "The spelling and grammar check is complete," click **OK**.

(continued on next page)

Once you spell-check a document or click **Ignore**, errors will no longer be marked, even if you spell-check the document again.

Note: Word will automatically correct some typical mistakes immediately after you type them—often without you being aware of it. For example, if you type "teh" and press the SPACE BAR, Word will automatically change it to "the" on the fly (try it).

Note: To see which words will be corrected automatically as you type, click the **Microsoft Office Button, Word Options**. In the **Word Options** window from the left pane, click the **Proofing** button; under **AutoCorrect options**, click the **AutoCorrect Options** button. From the **AutoCorrect** window, click the **AutoCorrect** tab. The items listed under the **Replace** column will be replaced with the items listed under the **With** column. Click the **Cancel** button twice to return to the Word document.

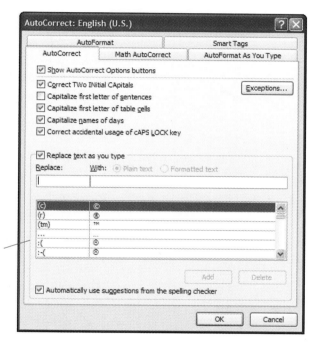

The keystrokes in the **Replace** box or column are automatically replaced with those in the **With** box or column as soon as you press the SPACE BAR.

You can add to or delete items from this list as desired.

Even the spelling-checker, however, will not always identify omitted words, misused words, or typographical errors that form a new word (such as "sing" for "sign"). Thus, you should always proofread your documents manually before submitting them.

(continued on next page)

PRACTICE *(continued)*

1. Type this sentence after the last line in this paragraph: Usage costs is a significant factor to be studied carefully. Next, press **CTRL + HOME** to move to the top of the document; then note the words marked with a red, wavy underline and a green, wavy underline.

> To evaluate the potential usge times for incoming calls to Rufty Company, a data phone log was kept for the week of November 13-17. For each incoming phone call, the total time in minutes of the phone call and the half hour in which the phone call was received was recorded. This data provided the usage time four assessing the costs of a toll-free service for Rufty. By recording when the calls were received, the numberof incoming lines could be evaluated. A telephone interview with an AT&T representative also assisted in eliminating usage costs, line costs, and equipment costs. Usage costs is a significant factor to be studied carefully.

2. From the **Review** tab, **Proofing** group, click the **Spelling & Grammar** button, or on the keyboard, press **F7**.
   a. Word displays the word "usge" in the **Not in Dictionary** box and suggests the word "usage" instead. Click **Change** to accept this suggestion.
   b. Word displays "Rufty" in the **Not in Dictionary** box and suggests the word "Rutty" instead. However, the word "Rufty" is correct, and it occurs throughout the document. Click **Ignore All** so that Word will not mark this word again. Instead of clicking **Ignore All**, you could click **Add** to add the word to Word's custom dictionary.
   c. Word displays "numberof" in the **Not in Dictionary** box and provides a suggested spelling. Click the correct suggestion. Then click **Change**.

   Note: To remove a word from the dictionary when you add it by mistake, do this: Click the **Microsoft Office Button**, and click the **Word Options** button. From the left pane, click **Proofing**. From the right pane under **When correcting spelling in Microsoft Office programs**, click **Custom Dictionaries**. From the **Custom Dictionaries** window, click **Edit Word List**. From the **CUSTOM.DIC** window, under the **Dictionary** box, click the desired word, click **Delete**, and click **OK** three times.

   d. Word displays "Usage costs is" in the **Subject-Verb Agreement** box and displays a suggestion in the **Suggestions** box. This suggestion is correct, so click **Change**. If you aren't sure if the suggestion is correct, you could click **Explain**.
   e. When Word displays the dialog box with the message "The spelling and grammar check is complete," click **OK**.
   f. Manually proofread the document after running the spell-checker. Note that one error has **not** been corrected. In line 4, the word "four" should be "for." Because "four" is in Word's internal dictionary, it was not marked. Change "four" to "for."

(continued on next page)

Your lines should now look like the following illustration:

> To evaluate the potential usage times for incoming calls to Rufty Company, a data phone log was kept for the week of November 13-17. For each incoming phone call, the total time in minutes of the phone call and the half hour in which the phone call was received was recorded. This data provided the usage time for assessing the costs of a toll-free service for Rufty. By recording when the calls were received, the number of incoming lines could be evaluated. A telephone interview with an AT&T representative also assisted in eliminating usage costs, line costs, and equipment costs. Usage costs are a significant factor to be studied carefully.

3. Save the document.

Note: Keep this document open and continue reading below.

Show Formatting

When you press a nonprinting key such as TAB or ENTER, Word inserts a formatting mark into the document. For example, pressing ENTER inserts a paragraph mark (¶) and starts a new paragraph; and pressing **TAB** inserts a tab character (→) and indents the line. Word defines a *paragraph* as any text or graphic that is followed by a ¶ mark. Pressing ENTER is also referred to as inseting a "hard return."

To see exactly where a paragraph ends or how many spaces you inserted, display the formatting marks.

To view formatting marks on the screen:

1. From the **Home** tab, **Paragraph** group, click the **Show/Hide** button

Show/Hide ¶ button

> **Or:** On the keyboard, press **CTRL + SHIFT + 8**.
> **Note:** On the keyboard, press **SHIFT + F1** to display the **Reveal Formatting** pane with detailed formatting information.
> The document now displays all of the formatting marks. Even though the formatting marks are displayed on the screen, they will not appear on the printed document.

Tab character (→)

Space character (•)

Paragraph mark (¶)

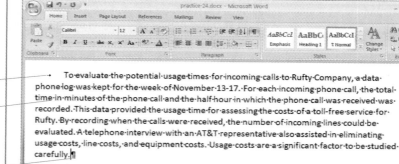

(continued on next page)

PRACTICE *(continued)*

1. From the **Home** tab, **Paragraph** group, click the **Show/Hide** button or press **CTRL + SHIFT + 8** to display the formatting marks.
2. Point to the different formatting marks shown on the screen such as the tab character, space character, and paragraph mark.
3. From the **Home** tab, **Paragraph** group, click the **Show/Hide** button or press **CTRL + SHIFT + 8** to hide the formatting marks.
4. Select the text "November 13-17" and apply bold and underline formatting.

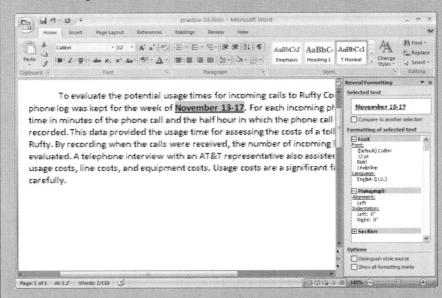

5. With the bold underlined text still selected, press **SHIFT + F1**.
6. Read the information in the **Reveal Formatting** task pane on the right of your screen.
7. Close the **Reveal Formatting** task pane.

Note: Keep this document open and continue on the next page.

(continued on next page)

Print

It is always a good idea to save a document before printing it. That way, if your printer causes a problem, you will not lose any of your work.

To print the document displayed on the screen:

1. Click the **Microsoft Office Button**, click the list arrow to the right of the **Print** button, and click **Print** or **Quick Print** as desired.

Or: On the keyboard, press **CTRL + P**.

Note: You will also see **GDP** as a choice under the **Microsoft Office Button** when you access Word via GDP.

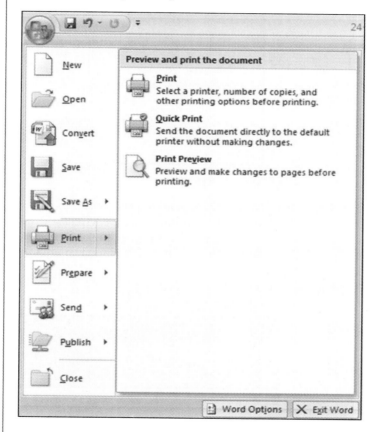

(continued on next page)

2. If you click **Print** or use the shortcut keystrokes, click the desired print options from the **Print** window. If you click **Quick Print**, you will print one copy of the entire document on your default printer.

Click **Current page** to print just the page containing the insertion point.

Click **Pages**, and type the page range if you want to print only certain pages (for example, typing "2-4" would cause pages 2 through 4 of a document to print).

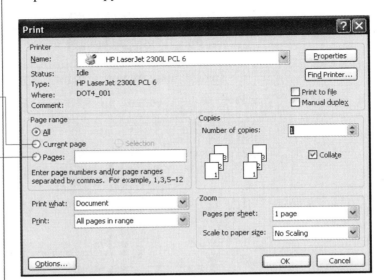

3. Click **OK**.

Note: If you want to print only a part of a document, first select the part you want to print. Click the **Microsoft Office Button**, point to the **Print** button, and click **Print** or press **CTRL + P**. Under **Page range**, click **Selection**, which will now be available.

PRACTICE *(continued)*

Note: Check with your instructor before printing anything.

1. Print two copies of this document.
2. Save changes to *practice-24*, and return to GDP.

Textbook

E-mail Basics

E-mail a Document

The e-mail feature in Word allows you to send a Word document as either the body of an e-mail message or as an attachment to an e-mail. The functionality of this e-mail feature depends upon what software you use for e-mail, what browser you use, and other factors that are beyond the scope of this manual. Generally speaking, if you use a Microsoft product for e-mail such as Outlook, Outlook Express, or Hotmail, you should be able to use this feature. In this lesson, you will review the steps to send a Word document as the actual e-mail message or to send a Word document as an e-mail attachment.

To send an open Word document as the actual e-mail message, you need to first add the **Send to Mail Recipient** command to the **Quick Access Toolbar**:

E-mail button

1. Open the desired Word file.
2. Click the list arrow next to the **Quick Access Toolbar** and click **More Commands**.
3. With **Customize** selected in the left pane, click the list arrow in the **Choose commands from list** box in the right pane, and click **All Commands**.
4. Scroll down the list, and click **Send to Mail Recipient**.
5. Click **Add** to add the command to the **Quick Access Toolbar;** click **OK**.

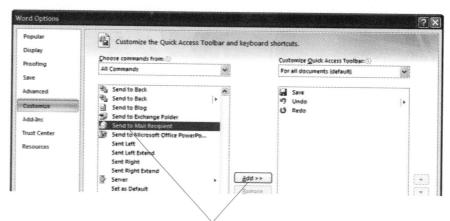

Click **Send to Mail Recipient** and then click **Add** to add the command to the **Quick Access Toolbar.**

(continued on next page)

6. With the desired Word file open, from the **Quick Access Toolbar**, click the **Send to Mail Recipient** button. Your Microsoft e-mail client will open.

7. Fill in the boxes as desired and send the e-mail as directed in your e-mail software.

Note: To remove the **Send to Mail Recipient** button from the **Quick Access Toolbar**, right-click the button and click **Remove from Quick Access Toolbar**.

To send an open Word document as an e-mail attachment:

1. Open the desired Word file.

2. Click the **Microsoft Office Button**, point to the arrow next to **Send**, and then click **E-mail**. Your Microsoft e-mail client will open.

Click **E-mail** to send a Word document as an attachment.

Note: You will also see **GDP** as a choice under the **Microsoft Office Button** when you access Word via GDP.

3. Fill in the boxes in your e-mail as desired and send the e-mail as directed in your e-mail software.

Note: Document processing begins in Lesson 25. You have access to a handy electronic Reference Manual when you are inside GDP and also when you are typing a document processing job inside Word. To access the electronic Reference Manual from inside Word, do this:

(continued on next page)

- Click the **Microsoft Office Button**, point to the arrow next to **GDP**, and click **Reference Manual**.
- When the manual opens, in the **GDP Reference Manual** window, click the **Contents** tab, and click the book icon to expand the contents list.
- Scroll down and click **E-mail Message in Microsoft Outlook/Internet Explorer**.
- Click each numbered blue callout and read any detailed formatting information.
- Click the **Index** tab and type a keyword in the **Type in keyword to find** box to search for a particular feature in any document and click **Display**.
- Click the **Search** tab, type a keyword in the **Type in keyword to find** box to search for a particular feature in any document, and click **List Topics**. Click the desired topic in the **Select topic to display** box, and click **Display**.
- Press **ALT + TAB** to cycle back and forth between your Word document or GDP and the electronic Reference Manual.
- Click the **Close** button (the "X" in the upper-right-hand corner of the window) to close the Reference Manual.

PRACTICE

Note: Check with your instructor before attempting to e-mail a document. **Note:** Because the functionality of Word's e-mail features depends upon what software you use for e-mail, what browser you use, and other factors that are beyond the scope of this manual, you will not actually send this e-mail message. Instead, refer to the start of this lesson for the steps you would normally take to send a Word document as the actual e-mail message or to send a Word document as an e-mail attachment.

1. Insert blank lines in *practice-25.docx* as needed to arrange the e-mail message in correct format as shown in Lesson 25 in the textbook.

   Note: E-mail addresses are normally converted to hyperlinks when you press a space after typing the e-mail address. However, GDP has set this default to off. See the Getting Started section in this manual for details.

2. If you were to send this Word document as the actual e-mail message with Outlook as your e-mail software, your message might look similar to this:

(continued on next page)

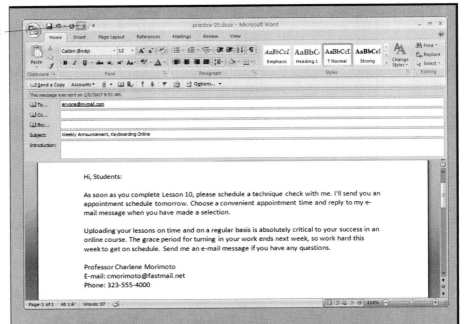

3. Click the **Microsoft Office Button**, point to the arrow next to **GDP**, and click **Reference Manual**.

4. When the manual opens, in the **GDP Reference Manual** window, click the **Contents** tab, and click the book icon to expand the contents list.

5. Scroll down and click **E-mail Message in Microsoft Outlook/ Internet Explorer**.

6. Click each numbered blue callout in the pane on the right, and read any detailed formatting information.

7. Click the **Index** tab, type `e-mail` in the **Type in keyword to find** box, and click **Display**.

8. Click the **Search** tab, type `writer's identification` in the **Type in keyword to find** box, and click **List Topics**.

9. Click each topic in the **Select topic to display** box, and click **Display** to view each one.

10. Press **ALT + TAB** to cycle back and forth between your Word document or GDP and the electronic Reference Manual.

11. Click the **Close** button (the "X" in the upper-right-hand corner of the window) to close the electronic Reference Manual.

12. Save changes to *practice-25*, and return to GDP.

Textbook

One-Page Business Reports

Alignment

Left alignment is the default setting.

Alignment buttons:

Word provides four ways of aligning text between the left and right margins:

- *Left:* Aligns text flush with the left margin, leaving an uneven right edge.
- *Right:* Aligns text flush with the right margin, leaving an uneven left edge.
- *Centered:* Centers the text between the left and right margins.
- *Justified:* Aligns text flush with both the left and the right margins.

To change the alignment of text:

1. From the **Home** tab, **Paragraph** group, click the desired alignment button.

   Or: From the **Home** tab, click the **Paragraph Dialog Box Launcher**.

   - Click the down arrow in the **Alignment box**, and click the desired alignment. (Be sure the **Indents and Spacing** tab is active.)
   - Click **OK**.

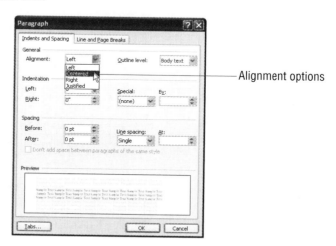

Alignment options

   Or: On the keyboard, press:

   - **CTRL + L** for left alignment.
   - **CTRL + E** for center alignment.

(continued on next page)

- **CTRL + R** for right alignment.
- **CTRL + J** for justified alignment.

PRACTICE

1. With the insertion point at the beginning of the document, press **ENTER** 2 times; then move the insertion point back to the beginning of the document.
2. Type DRAFT centered in all caps and bold, and turn on **Show/Hide**.
3. In the first line of paragraph 1, change increased to increase in the.
4. All paragraphs are now shown with left alignment. Change paragraph 2 to justified alignment.
5. Change paragraph 3 to right alignment.
   Your document should now look like this:

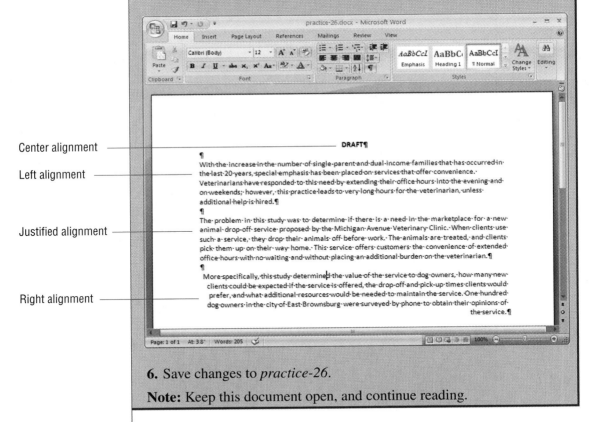

Center alignment

Left alignment

Justified alignment

Right alignment

6. Save changes to *practice-26*.

Note: Keep this document open, and continue reading.

(continued on next page)

Font Size

Font sizes are measured in *points*; 1 point (abbreviated *pt*) is equal to 1/72 of an inch. The point size refers to the height of a character. Thus, a 12-pt font is 1/6 inch in height.

Shown below are some examples of different font sizes you can use.

10-point Font Size

12-point Font Size

18-point Font Size

24-point Font Size

You can easily change the font size in your text. Avoid, however, using too many font sizes in the same document.

To change font size:

1. Position the insertion point where you want to begin using the new font size (or select the text you want to change).
2. From the **Home** tab, **Font** group, click the down arrow to the right of the **Font Size** box, and click the desired font size.

   Or: Click the **Grow Font** or **Shrink Font** buttons as desired.
   Or: On the keyboard, press **CTRL + D**. Click the **Font** tab if necessary. When the **Font** window appears, click the desired font size; then click **OK**.

Note: GDP has changed the default font from Calibri 11 to Calibri 12. See the Getting Started section in this manual for details.

Font Size box

Grow Font button

Shrink Font button

You can change the font size through the **Font** dialog box.

(continued on next page)

PRACTICE *(continued)*

1. Move the insertion point to the top of the document, and press **ENTER** 5 times to begin the report title 2 inches from the top of the page.
2. Select the word DRAFT and change the font size to 14 points; look at the **Vertical Page Position** bar on the status bar and verify that the insertion point is at 2".
3. Move the insertion point just after DRAFT, press **ENTER** 2 times, type July 1, 20--, and bold it if necessary.
4. Select the date you just typed, and change the font size to 12 points.
5. Change the justification in all paragraphs to left alignment.
6. Press **ENTER** 2 times after the first paragraph, and move the insertion point up one line.
7. Type the side heading PROBLEM, and bold the heading. Your document should look like this.

Note that the insertion point is positioned in the line where the report title is typed. Therefore, when you look at the **Vertical Page position** bar on the status bar, you can verify that you are **At: 2"** (2 inches from the top of the page).

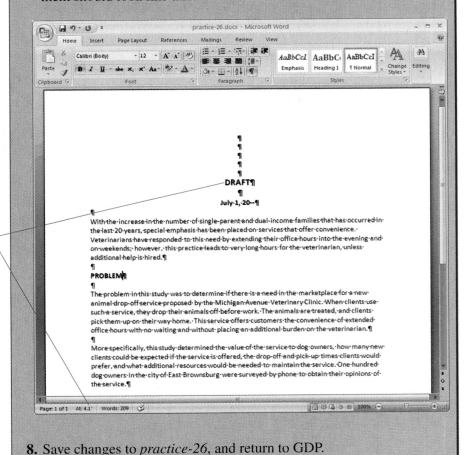

8. Save changes to *practice-26*, and return to GDP.

Go To Textbook

Multipage Business Reports

Page Numbering

Use the **Page Number** command to insert the correct page number in the upper-right-hand corner of each page. You can also remove the page number from the first page of the document.

To see page numbers on the screen, be sure you are in **Print Layout** view. To switch to **Print Layout** view, click the **Print Layout** view button on the status bar.

Note: Before you begin the steps below, do this: From the **Page Layout** tab, click the **Page Setup Dialog Box Launcher**, and then click the **Layout** tab. Under **Headers and footers**, verify that **Different first page** is *unchecked*; click **OK**.

To insert a page number in the top right-hand corner of the page header and remove the page number from the first page:

1. From the **Insert** tab, **Header & Footer** group, click **Page Number**.
2. Click **Top of Page** (or **Bottom of Page** or **Page Margins** depending on the desired position for the page number).
3. Click **Plain Number 3** from the gallery of designs to position the page number in the top right-hand corner of the page or click the desired page numbering design from the gallery of designs. You should now be inside the **Header** section with the document dimmed.

Print Layout View button

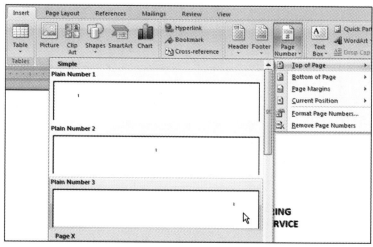

(continued on next page)

---

4. From the **Page Layout** tab, click the **Page Setup Dialog Box Launcher**, and then click the **Layout** tab. Under **Headers and footers**, check **Different first page**; click **OK**. You should now be in the **First Page Header** section and the page number should be gone.

   Note: If the page number is still in the **First Page Header**, select the page number and cut it.

5. Double-click anywhere outside the **First Page Header** area inside the document area to close the header and to return to the document; or from the **Design** tab, **Close** group, click the **Close Header and Footer** button. The header should now be dimmed and the document should be active. Note that the first page header is blank and the second page now has a page number.

6. Double-click anywhere inside the header to reopen it.

Note: To remove the page number on the first page of your document *after* you have returned to the document, do this: Click inside the desired page. From the **Page Layout** tab, click the **Page Setup Dialog Box Launcher**, and then click the **Layout** tab. Under **Headers and footers**, check **Different first page**; click **OK**.

Note: To start numbering pages with a different number, click anywhere in the document. From the **Insert** tab, in the **Header & Footer** group, click **Page Number**. Click **Format Page Numbers**. In the **Start at** box, type the desired number; click **OK**.

Note: To remove page numbers entirely, from the **Insert** tab, in the **Header & Footer** group, click **Page Number**. Click **Remove Page Numbers**. Do this on both the first and second pages of the document if you have turned off page numbering on the first page.

(continued on next page)

PRACTICE

1. Use the **Page Number** command to automatically insert page numbers at the top right of each page. (If necessary, switch to **Print Layout** view.)
2. Remove the page number from page 1.
3. Print the document or use **Print Preview** to ensure that the page numbers are positioned correctly.

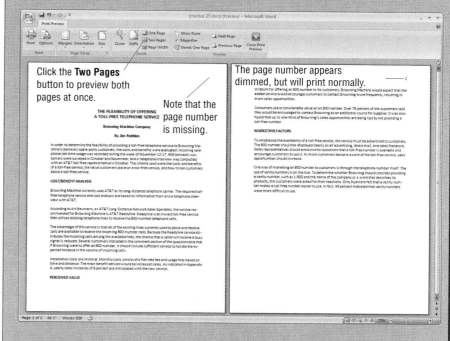

Click the **Two Pages** button to preview both pages at once.

Note that the page number is missing.

The page number appears dimmed, but will print normally.

4. Save changes to *practice-27*.

Note: Keep this document open, and continue reading on the next page.

(continued on next page)

Page Break

As you type, Word automatically starts an additional page when the current page is filled. The page break can move, depending upon whether text is added to or deleted from the page. The status bar also changes to reflect which page of the document the insertion point is in.

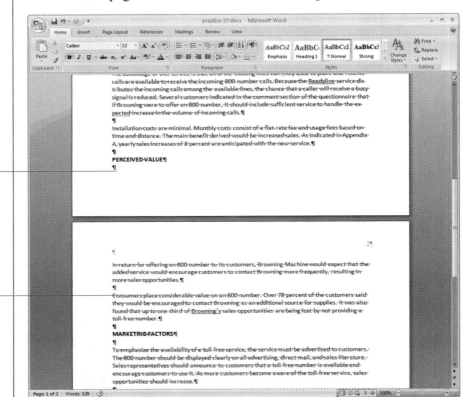

Never end a page with a single line (one line of a heading or one line of a new paragraph), also known as an orphan.

Never begin a page with a single line (the last line of a paragraph from the previous page), also known as widow. The break shown here is acceptable because the page begins with at least two lines of the paragraph

(continued on next page)

To avoid leaving a single line at the bottom or top of a page, you would force a page to end at a particular spot by inserting a *manual page break*. No matter what text is added to or deleted from the document, the page will end at this point unless you later delete the manual page break.

To insert a manual page break:

1. From the **Home** tab, in the **Paragraph** group, click **Show/Hide** so that you will be able to see the **Page Break** formatting symbol.
2. Click where you want to start a new page.
3. From the **Insert** tab, in the **Pages** group, click **Page Break**.

Or: On the keyboard, press **CTRL + ENTER**.

Note: The manual page break in the illustration was inserted to avoid leaving the side heading as a single line at the bottom of the first page.

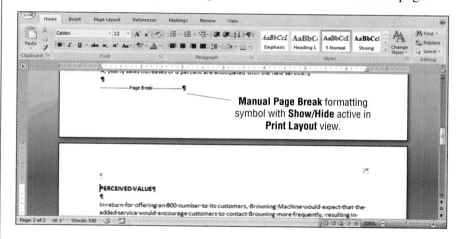

Manual Page Break formatting symbol with **Show/Hide** active in **Print Layout** view.

PRACTICE *(continued)*

1. Change to **Print Layout** view; then move the insertion point immediately in front of the side heading *PERCEIVED VALUE*.
2. Insert a manual page break, and turn on **Show/Hide**.
3. Save changes to *practice-27*.
4. Return to GDP.

Go To   **Textbook**

Bulleted and Numbered Lists

Bullets and Numbering

Numbering
button

Bullets
button

To insert a line break within a bulleted or numbered list (for example, to add a blank line or an explanatory note that begins on a separate line), press SHIFT + ENTER.

To call attention to a list of items, you might want to format them with bullets or with numbers. If the sequence of the items in the list is important, use numbers; if not, use bullets. The numbers or bullets are automatically indented from the left margin but may be repositioned, as you will see later.

To add bullets or numbers:

1. Press **ENTER** as needed to insert 1 blank line above the list; then position the insertion point where you want the bullets or numbers to begin.
2. Type your list of items *unformatted* (without the bullets or numbers) at the left margin; then press **ENTER** as needed to insert a blank line below the list. (Remember, if any items in the list are multiline, insert a blank line between the items for readability.)

   Note: If an indented paragraph immediately follows a list, type both the list **and** the indented paragraph **before** you apply bullets or numbers to ensure that a succeeding paragraph is indented correctly when you press TAB.

3. Select the text to be formatted with bullets or numbers.
4. From the **Home** tab, **Paragraph** group, click either the **Bullets** or **Numbering** button.

   Or: From the **Home** tab, **Paragraph** group, click the list arrow next to either the **Bullets** or **Numbering** button; then click the desired bullet or numbering format from one of the libraries.

Note: To change the number of the list so that it starts with a particular number, select the list items, right-click, and click **Set Line Numbering Value**. Click **Start new list** to start again at 1. Click **Continue from previous list** to continue numbering for a preceding list. Or type the desired number in the **Set value to** box, and click **OK**. You might need to click the **Numbering** button twice right after this to reset the line number value on the selected lines.

Note: To avoid unwanted indentions when you have to press the TAB or BACKSPACE key after typing a list, you can change the following Word setting: Click the **Microsoft Office Button**, **Word Options**. From the **Word Options** window, click **Proofing** in the left pane, and click the **AutoCorrect Options** button on the right. In the **AutoCorrect** window, click the **AutoFormat As You Type** tab, and uncheck **Set left- and first-indent with tabs and backspaces.** Click **OK** twice.

(continued on next page)

To remove bullets or numbers, select the desired list and click either the **Bullets** or **Numbering** button.

DECREASE INDENT

Decrease Indent button

By default, Word indents a bulleted or numbered list. However, numbers and bullets should appear at the left margin in a document with blocked paragraphs. Use the **Decrease Indent** button from the **Home** tab, **Paragraph** group, to position the list at the left margin.

To position a list at the left margin:

1. Create the bulleted or numbered list as explained in Steps 1–4.
2. Select the list.
3. From the **Home** tab, **Paragraph** group, click the **Decrease Indent** button to position the list at the left margin in a blocked document.

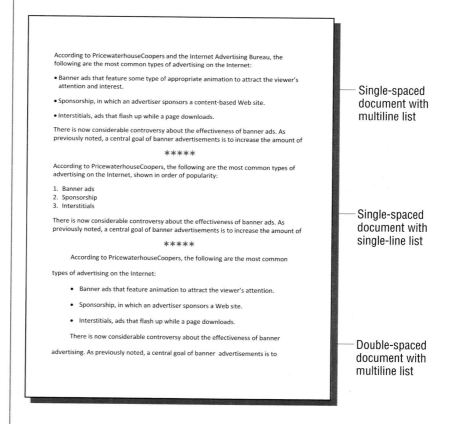

According to PricewaterhouseCoopers and the Internet Advertising Bureau, the following are the most common types of advertising on the Internet:

- Banner ads that feature some type of appropriate animation to attract the viewer's attention and interest.
- Sponsorship, in which an advertiser sponsors a content-based Web site.
- Interstitials, ads that flash up while a page downloads.

There is now considerable controversy about the effectiveness of banner ads. As previously noted, a central goal of banner advertisements is to increase the amount of

*****

— Single-spaced document with multiline list

According to PricewaterhouseCoopers, the following are the most common types of advertising on the Internet, shown in order of popularity:

1. Banner ads
2. Sponsorship
3. Interstitials

There is now considerable controversy about the effectiveness of banner ads. As previously noted, a central goal of banner advertisements is to increase the amount of

*****

— Single-spaced document with single-line list

According to PricewaterhouseCoopers, the following are the most common types of advertising on the Internet:

- Banner ads that feature animation to attract the viewer's attention.
- Sponsorship, in which an advertiser sponsors a Web site.
- Interstitials, ads that flash up while a page downloads.

There is now considerable controversy about the effectiveness of banner advertising. As previously noted, a central goal of banner advertisements is to

— Double-spaced document with multiline list

(continued on next page)

PRACTICE

1. Format the sentences in the illustration that end with question marks as a numbered list; then decrease the indent to position the numbered list at the left margin. (Remember to select the sentences.)

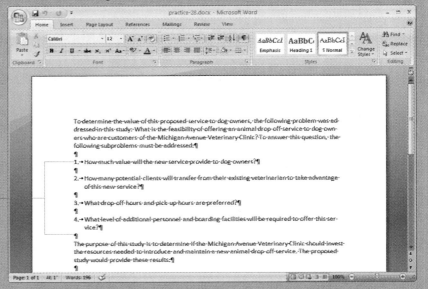

Type a list unformatted and type any paragraph immediately following the list. Then go back, select the list, and convert it to a numbered or bulleted list.

2. Move the insertion point to the end of the document (Hint: **CTRL + END**), and type the following text, press **ENTER** 1 time between sentences, and press **ENTER** 2 times before the last sentence.

   Provide a better understanding of the need for this service.
   Define some of the mechanics of the service.
   Provide direction on how to introduce this service.
   Although cat owners also represent a large client base for the veterinarian, they were excluded from this study because cats do not have to be licensed.

3. Select the three single-line sentences above the last paragraph and apply bullets to the list.
4. With the list still selected, position the list at the left margin.
5. Use **Print Preview** to see how your document will look when it is printed.

(continued on next page)

For single-spaced documents, if any item requires more than one line, single-space each item but insert a blank line.

For single-spaced documents, if all items require no more than one line, single-space the items in the list.

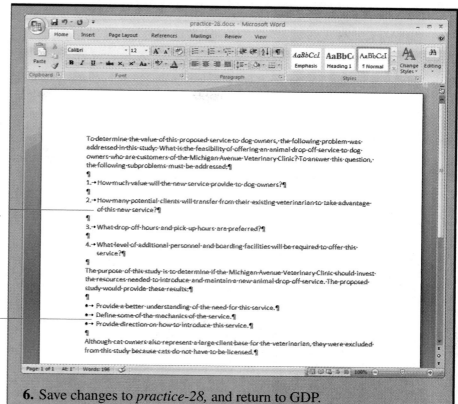

Go To Textbook

6. Save changes to *practice-28*, and return to GDP.

Academic Reports

Line Spacing

You can easily change the line spacing from single to 1.5 line spacing (which adds an extra half line of space between typed lines) or to double-spacing (which adds an extra blank line between typed lines). The precise amount of space between lines is determined by the size of the font you are using.

Note: GDP has set the default line spacing from multiple-line spacing to single-line spacing and the default spacing after paragraphs from 10 pt to 0 pt. See the Getting Started section in this manual for details.

To change line spacing:

1. Move the insertion point into the paragraph you want to change (or select the paragraphs you want to change).
2. From the **Home** tab, click the **Paragraph Dialog Box Launcher**. From the **Paragraph** window, click the **Indents and Spacing** tab.
3. Click the down arrow in the **Line spacing** list box, and click the desired line spacing option.

Line spacing button

Line spacing options

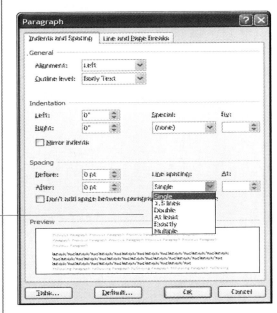

(continued on next page)

4. Click **OK**.

Or: On the keyboard, press:

- **CTRL+1** for single spacing
- **CTRL+5** for 1.5 spacing
- **CTRL+2** for double spacing

Or: From the **Home** tab, **Paragraph** group, click the list arrow on the **Line spacing** button, and click the desired line spacing option.

When you click the list arrow on the **Line spacing** button, you will see a check by the current line spacing

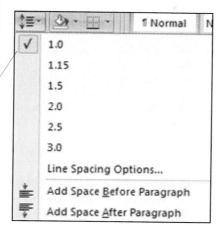

Note: If you change line spacing at the beginning of a document, all paragraphs that you type will reflect the new spacing unless you change the spacing again. If you change the line spacing in an existing paragraph, only the lines of that paragraph are changed.

To change line spacing for an entire document that has already been typed:

1. Press **CTRL+A** to select the entire document.
2. Follow steps 1–4 on pages 58 and 59 or use the keyboard shortcut keys listed above.

(continued on next page)

PRACTICE

1. Select the entire document with **CTRL+A**, and press **CTRL+2** to change to double-spacing.
2. Turn on **Show/Hide** and delete the extra blank lines above, between, and below the lines of the numbered list.
3. Delete the extra blank line above and below the bulleted list.
4. Click in front of each of the paragraphs, and press **TAB** to indent the paragraphs.
5. Select the numbered and bulleted lists one at a time, and increase the indent until the lists are aligned with the paragraph indents. (*Hint:* Either click the **Increase Indent** button 2 times; or click the **Numbering** or **Bullets** button 2 times to remove and then apply numbers or bullets, and click the **Increase Indent** button once.) Your document should look similar to this:

> → To·determine·the·value·of·this·proposed·service·to·dog·owners,·the·following·problem·
> was·addressed·in·this·study:·What·is·the·feasibility·of·offering·an·animal·drop-off·service·to·dog·
> owners·who·are·customers·of·the·Michigan·Avenue·Veterinary·Clinic?·To·answer·this·question,·
> the·following·subproblems·must·be·addressed:¶
>
> 1.→How·much·value·will·the·new·service·provide·to·dog·owners?¶
>
> 2.→How·many·potential·clients·will·transfer·from·their·existing·veterinarian·to·take·
> advantage·of·this·new·service?¶
>
> 3.→What·drop-off·hours·and·pick-up·hours·are·preferred?¶
>
> 4.→What·level·of·additional·personnel·and·boarding·facilities·will·be·required·to·offer·
> this·service?¶
>
> → The·purpose·of·this·study·is·to·determine·if·the·Michigan·Avenue·Veterinary·Clinic·
> should·invest·the·resources·needed·to·introduce·and·maintain·a·new·animal·drop-off·service.·
> The·proposed·study·would·provide·these·results:¶
>
> •→Provide·a·better·understanding·of·the·need·for·this·service.¶
>
> •→Define·some·of·the·mechanics·of·the·service.¶
>
> •→Provide·direction·on·how·to·introduce·this·service.¶
>
> → Although·cat·owners·also·represent·a·large·client·base·for·the·veterinarian,·they·were·
> excluded·from·this·study·because·cats·do·not·have·to·be·licensed.¶

6. Save changes to *practice-29,* and return to GDP.

Go To Textbook

Academic Reports With Displays

Increase Indent

If the paragraphs in a document are indented, numbers and bulleted lists should be indented to the same point as the indented paragraphs. To position a list at the same point as an indented paragraph, use the **Increase Indent** button.

To position a list at the same position as an indented paragraph:

1. Type the list unformatted with appropriate spacing.
2. Select the list, and apply bullets or numbers.
3. From the **Home** tab, **Paragraph** group, click the **Increase Indent** button to position the selected list as desired.

   Or: Right-click the selected list and click the **Increase Indent** button to position the list as desired.

Note: If you indent the list too much, click the **Decrease Indent** button as needed.

Increase Indent button

DOUBLE INDENT

Paragraphs can be indented from both the left and right margins (double indent) to set off a quoted paragraph having 4 lines or more or a paragraph that needs special emphasis.

To format a displayed paragraph with a double indent:

1. Type the displayed paragraph and the paragraph immediately following it.
2. Select only the lines to be included in the displayed paragraph and change the line spacing to single.

   Note: In a single-spaced report, changing line spacing would not apply.

3. With the text still selected, from the **Home** tab, click the **Paragraph Dialog Box Launcher.**
4. If necessary, click the **Indents and Spacing** tab.

(continued on next page)

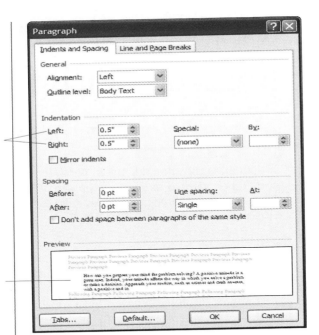

Indentation is typically set 0.5" from each margin.

Look in the **Preview** box to see the effect of each setting.

5. Under **Indentation**, click the arrows next to the **Left** and **Right** boxes to increase or decrease the paragraph indentation (typically 0.5 inch) from each margin.
6. Click **OK**.
7. Click immediately after the last period in the displayed paragraph, and press ENTER 1 time to insert 1 blank line after the displayed paragraph.

PRACTICE

1. Select the fifth paragraph ("How can you . . .") and change the line spacing to single.
2. Format the paragraph with a 0.5-inch double indent.
3. Turn on **Show/Hide**, click after the last character in the paragraph, and press ENTER 1 time to insert 1 blank line after the paragraph.

(continued on next page)

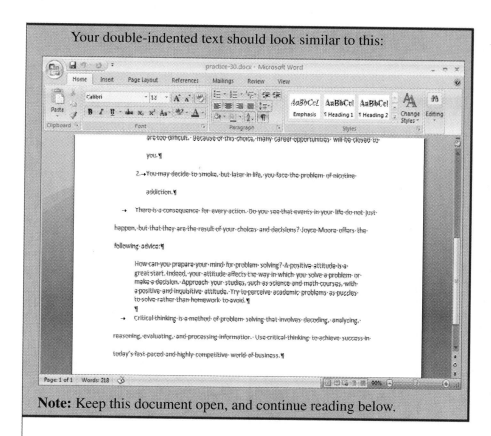

Your double-indented text should look similar to this:

Note: Keep this document open, and continue reading below.

Cut, Copy, and Paste

You can move or copy text from one part of a document to another. To *move* text means to first cut (delete) the selected text from one location and then paste (insert) it in another location (either in the same document or in a different document). To *copy* text means to make a copy of the selected text and then insert (paste) it in another location; copying leaves the original text unchanged.

The **Microsoft Office Clipboard** allows you to copy several items, such as text and pictures, from Office documents or other programs and paste them into another Office document. Each time you cut or copy an item, you add it to the collection of items in the **Clipboard**. You can click any item from the list of selected items to paste it into a different place in the current document or move to a new document and paste any item there. You can paste the same item repeatedly. When you exit all Office programs, the last item that you copied stays on the **Clipboard**. When you exit all Office programs and restart your computer, all items are cleared from the **Office Clipboard**.

Cut, Copy,
and **Paste**
buttons

(continued on next page)

To display the **Office Clipboard** in the left pane, from the **Home** tab, in the **Clipboard** group, click the **Clipboard Dialog Box Launcher**. You can also select some text to copy and press **CTRL + C** twice. Click any item under **Click an item to paste** to paste it into your document at the insertion point. Click the **Options** button to select any desired options for displaying the Clipboard. Click the **Clear All** button to clear the **Clipboard**. To close the **Clipboard**, click the **Close** button at the top of the pane.

To cut and paste (move) text:

1. From the **Home** tab, in the **Clipboard** group, click the **Clipboard Dialog Box Launcher** to display the **Office Clipboard**; in your document, select the text you want to move.

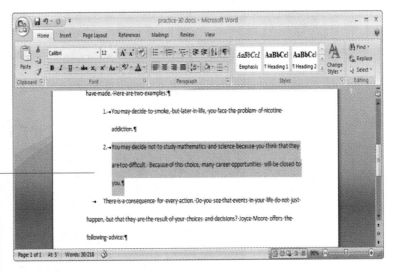

The sentence to be cut and pasted (moved) is selected (highlighted).

2. From the **Home** tab, **Clipboard** group, click the **Cut** button.

   Or: On the keyboard, press **CTRL + X**.

Note: When you paste text, you might see a **Paste Options** button appear just below your pasted selection. Press **Esc** to make the button disappear for that instance, or click the **Paste Options** button to choose a desired action from a list. Other choices may appear depending on the formatting of the source and destination text.

Paste Options button

(continued on next page)

- ***Keep Source Formatting:*** Pasted text will appear exactly as it did in the source.
- ***Match Destination Formatting:*** Pasted text will change itself to match the formatting of the surrounding text in the destination.
- ***Keep Text Only:*** All formatting will be removed from the pasted text and the pasted text will change itself to match the formatting of the surrounding text in the destination.

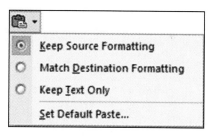

The selected sentence that was previously cut now appears in the **Clipboard** for pasting into any Office document.

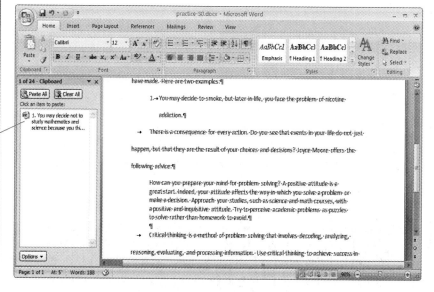

3. Position the insertion point where you want to insert the text.
4. From the **Home** tab, **Paragraph** group, click the **Paste** button to make the selected text reappear in its new location.

   Or: On the keyboard, press **CTRL + V**.
   Or: On the **Clipboard** pane, click the cut item.

Note: Always check the revised text to ensure that you moved exactly what you wanted to move and that the spacing, punctuation, and formatting are correct.

(continued on next page)

Note: To move text, you can also point to the selected text and drag and drop it into place in the desired location.

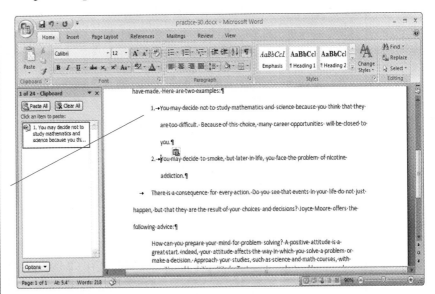

The selected sentence has been pasted from the **Clipboard** into its new location and renumbered

The keyboard shortcuts for **Cut (CTRL+X)**, **Copy (CTRL+C)**, and **Paste (CTRL+V)** can be used in any Windows program—for example, database or spreadsheet programs.

To copy and paste text:

1. From the **Home** tab, in the **Clipboard** group, click the **Clipboard Dialog Box Launcher** to display the **Clipboard** pane.
2. Select the text you want to copy. From the **Home** tab, **Clipboard** group, click the **Copy** button. You will see the copied text in the Clipboard pane.

   Or: On the keyboard, press **CTRL + C**.

3. Position the insertion point where you want to paste the copied text.
4. From the **Home** tab, **Clipboard** group, click the **Paste** button to make the selected text reappear in its new location.

   Or: On the keyboard, press **CTRL + V**.
   Or: On the **Clipboard** pane, click the copied item.

(continued on next page)

PRACTICE *(continued)*

1. Select the second and third paragraphs ("You may decide . . ."), apply numbers to them, click the **Decrease Indent** button once to change the number list level from letters to numbers, and click the **Increase Indent** button once to position the list so that these numbered paragraphs align with the paragraph indent. You will be transposing these paragraphs in the next few steps.

2. Make sure that **Show/Hide** is active, and select the second numbered paragraph ("You may decide not to study . . ."), being sure to include the paragraph symbol at the end of the paragraph.

   Note: You cannot select the paragraph number because it was created using the **Numbering** command rather than typing it manually.

3. Display the **Office Clipboard**, clear it, and cut the selected paragraph.

4. Click just before the first numbered paragraph in front of the "Y" in "You may decide to smoke . . ."

5. Paste the cut paragraph in this location.

   Note: The paragraphs are automatically renumbered after pasting.

6. Press **Esc** to make the **Paste Options** button disappear. Your document should look similar to the following screen:

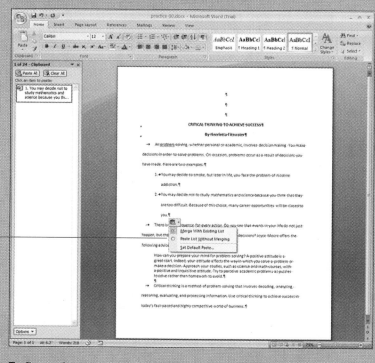

You should explore **Paste Options** whenever you paste as there are often helpful context-sensitive shortcuts for pasting text.

7. Save changes to *practice-30*, and return to GDP.

Business Letters

Insert Date

Word's **AutoComplete** feature helps you quickly insert calendar terms (such as the names of months and the names of days of the week). After you type the first four letters of a month with a long name such as January, Word displays a screen tip to help you complete the partially typed month.

To insert a month and year using **AutoComplete**:

1. Type the first four letters of any of these months: January, February, August, September, October, November, or December.
2. After you have typed the fourth letter and see a screen tip displaying the completed month and the direction to press Enter to insert the text, press **ENTER**.
3. Type the day of the month followed by a comma, and the current year should display.
4. Press **ENTER** to insert the current year.

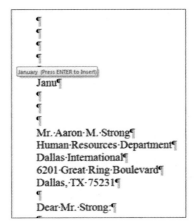

To insert the current date using **AutoComplete**:

1. Type the current month entirely.
2. Word will next display a screen tip with the complete current date; press **ENTER** to accept the current month, day, and year.

(continued on next page)

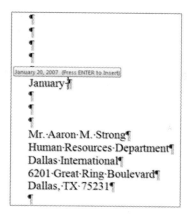

¶
¶
¶
¶
¶
January 20, 2007 (Press ENTER to Insert)
January·¶
¶
¶
¶
Mr.·Aaron·M.·Strong¶
Human·Resources·Department¶
Dallas·International¶
6201·Great·Ring·Boulevard¶
Dallas,·TX·75231¶
¶

Note: If you are typing a date in a form letter and you want to have the date change to the current date each time you send or open the form letter, you would insert the date using a field. To do this, click where you want to insert a date field. From the **Insert** tab, in the **Text** group, click **Quick Parts**, and then click **Field**. From the **Field** window, in the **Field names**, click **Date**. From the **Date formats** list, click the desired format and click **OK**. The current date will be inserted. If you need to update the field, click the field and click the **Update** button that appears.

PRACTICE

1. Place the insertion point at the beginning of the letter and press **ENTER** 5 times to position the date 2 inches from the top margin.
2. Delete the date line of the letter, and use the **AutoComplete** feature to insert January as the month.
3. After you type Janu, press **ENTER** to complete the word and then type a space followed by 14, a comma, and the current year.
4. At the bottom of the letter, select *urs* and type your own reference initials using the first initial of your first name and the first initial of your last name in lowercase letters without any spaces, and press **ENTER** 2 times.
5. Practice using the **AutoComplete** feature to insert the current date at the bottom of the letter; then delete any of these practice lines when you're finished.

Note: Word's **AutoCorrect** feature would normally capitalize the first letter of your reference initials when you either press **ENTER** or type a space after typing your reference initials because Word assumes that your first initial is the first letter of a sentence for that line. However, GDP has set this **AutoCorrect** option to off, so your capitalization will remain intact. See the Getting Started section in this manual for details. Remember that you can reverse any unwanted change by clicking **Undo** immediately after an undesirable change has been made.

6. Save changes to *practice-31*, and return to GDP.

Envelopes and Labels

Envelopes

Word makes it easy to format and print envelopes. In fact, if you type a letter first, Word can almost always identify the inside address and automatically insert it into the envelope window so that you don't have to retype it.

To insert an envelope:

1. From the **Mailings** tab, **Create** group, click the **Envelopes** button.
2. Click the **Envelopes** tab if necessary.

Word searches your current document for what "looks like" an inside address and inserts it into the **Delivery address** window.

A No. 10 envelope is the default setting. Click **Options** below the **Preview** window to select another envelope size.

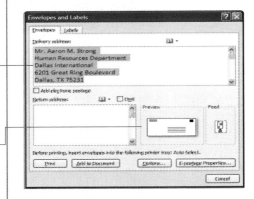

3. If you already typed a letter that included an inside address, the **Delivery address** box will already have the inside address inserted. Edit the address if necessary. If you did not first type a letter with an inside address, type the delivery address now.
4. Type a return address; or if you are using an envelope with a printed return address, be sure the **Return address** box is empty or click the **Omit** check box.
5. Insert an envelope in the correct position into your printer and click **Print**.

Note: If you want to save the envelope or if you need to change printers from the default printer, click **Add to Document**. Word adds (appends) the envelope to a blank document if you have not created a letter, or to the letter if you have one displayed on screen. Any time you print the letter, you will also print the envelope. You may need to make special adjustments to your printer in order to print an envelope.

(continued on next page)

PRACTICE

1. Press **ENTER** 5 times above the date and edit the date; from the **Mailings** tab, **Create** group, click the **Envelopes** button.
Your screen should look like this:

2. Insert a No. 10 envelope into the printer and print the envelope. Your printed envelope should look like this:

> Mr. Aaron M. Strong
> Human Resources Department
> Dallas International
> 6201 Great Ring Boulevard
> Dallas, TX 75231

Note: Check with your instructor before printing. As an alternative to printing, click **Add to Document**, and view the envelope at the top of the page.

3. From the **Microsoft Office Button**, click **Close**, but do not return to GDP. When prompted to save changes, click **No**.

(continued on next page)

Labels

It is easy to print labels to be used as a return address or a delivery address. You can print a full page of the same label or a single label. You can also choose from a variety of label sizes.

   To print a single label:

1. Open a new file.
2. From the **Mailings** tab, **Create** group, click the **Labels** button.
3. Click the **Labels** tab.

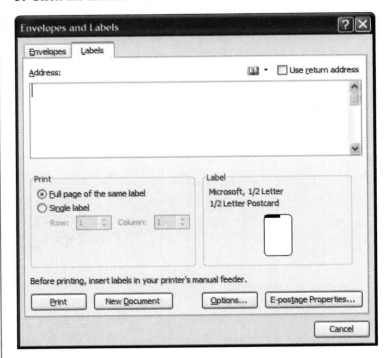

4. Type the mailing address in the **Address** box.

   Note: If you open the **Envelopes and Labels** dialog box with an active document, Word will search for an address and insert it automatically.

5. Clear the check box for **Use return address**, if necessary.
6. Click **Single label**.
7. Click the **Options** button.

(continued on next page)

Click the desired vendor from the **Label vendors** box.

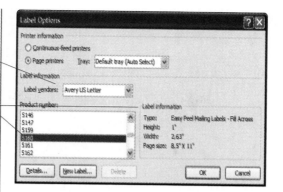

Click the desired product from the **Product number** box. Note the label details under **Label information**.

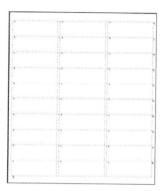

This is the blank label form for Avery US Letter 5160.

8. Under **Label vendors**, click **Avery US Letter**.
9. Under **Product number**, click **5160**; click **OK**.
10. Click **Print**.

To print a full page of the same label:

1. Open a new file.
2. From the **Mailings** tab, **Create** group, click the **Labels** button.
3. Click the **Labels** tab.
4. Type the mailing address in the **Address** box.
5. Clear the check box for **Use return address**, if necessary.
6. Click **Full page of the same label**.
7. Click the **Options** button.
8. Under **Label vendors**, click **Avery US Letter**; under **Product number**, click **5160**; click **OK**.

Note: You can choose any appropriate label as needed.

9. Click **New Document**.
10. Print the document.
11. Close the document. When prompted to save changes, choose **No**.

Note: To create a page of labels with different information on each label, skip step 4 above and delete any text that might appear in the **Address** box. After completing step 9, type the different label information in each separate box of the blank label form as desired.

PRACTICE *(continued)*

1. Open a new Word file. (*Hint:* Press **CTRL + N**.)
2. Open the **Envelopes and Labels** dialog box.
3. Click the **Labels** tab.
4. Delete any text that might appear in the **Address** box.
5. Clear the check box for **Use return address**, if necessary.

(continued on next page)

6. Click **Full page of the same label**.
7. Click the **Options** button.
8. Under **Label vendors**, click **Avery US Letter**; under **Product number**, click **5160**; click **OK**.
9. Click **New Document**. A full page of empty labels appears.
10. Type the following information in the first label.
    ```
    Ms. Renee Milfuggia
    Stevenson Corporation
    1479 Monroe Street
    Gastonia, NC 28054
    ```
11. Press **TAB** twice or click in the next label (middle label in first row) and type the following information.
    ```
    Mr. George Shawley
    1014 South Marietta Street
    Grove City, PA 16127
    ```
12. Print the document, if directed by your instructor.
13. Close the document. When prompted to save changes, click **No**.
14. Return to GDP.

Textbook

Correspondence Review

Italic and Underline

Italic button   **Underline** button

plain text

italic text

<u>underlined text</u>

Reminder: Another way to emphasize text is to format it in bold.

One way to emphasize text is to format the text in italic or to underline text. Because hyperlinks are commonly displayed with an underline, use italic rather than underlining in book titles, etc., to avoid confusing underlined text with hyperlinked text.

To italicize or underline text as you type:

1. From the **Home** tab, **Font** group, click the **Italic** or **Underline** button.

   Or: On the keyboard, press **CTRL+I** (italic) or **CTRL+U** (underline).

2. Type the text you want to appear italicized or underlined.
3. Click the **Italic** or **Underline** button again to turn off italic or underline. The text appears on screen in italic or underline.

   To italicize or underline existing text:

1. Select the text to be italicized or underlined.
2. Click the **Italic** or **Underline** button or press **CTRL+I** or **CTRL+U**.

Note: Italic and **Underline** are toggle buttons. Clicking the button once turns the feature on; clicking the button twice in succession turns the feature on and then off. If you italicize or underline text by accident, select the text and then click the desired button.

(continued on next page)

PRACTICE

1. Type the following paragraph exactly as it appears (but let word wrap end your lines for you):

   I will <u>not</u> have time to read *To Kill a Mockingbird* before Friday. I will have time to read This Old House.

2. In the second sentence, underline the word "will" and italicize the title "This Old House."

3. In the first sentence, delete the underline from the word "not."

   Your lines should now look like this:

   I will <u>not</u> have time to read *To Kill a Mockingbird* before Friday. I will have time to read *This Old House*.

Go To ▶ Textbook

4. Save changes to *practice-35*, and return to GDP.

Boxed Tables

Table—Insert

When you insert a table, Word applies borders by default. A table with borders is referred to as a boxed table, and a table without borders is an open table. You will learn to remove borders in a later lesson. A *table* consists of columns and rows displayed on screen with or without borders. Columns run from top to bottom, and rows run from left to right. A *cell* is the intersection of a row and a column. When you type text in a cell, the text can wrap to the next line of the cell, just as in a regular document. The cell expands vertically to make room for the next line.

Note: If you notice that the default font size inside a table is set to 11 pt rather than 12 pt, see the Getting Started section in this manual for steps to change the default font size.

The vertical columns are labeled by letters, and the horizontal rows are labeled by numbers. Thus, the practice table below has two columns (labeled A and B) and five rows (labeled 1 through 5). Thus "President" is located in Cell A1, the intersection of Column A and Row 1.

	A	B
1	President	Juanita Cortes-Perin
2	Vice President	Paul J. Anchor
3	Secretary	Rhetta Jones
4	Treasurer	Imogene Corker
5	Faculty Sponsor	Professor Leon South

Insert Table button

To insert a table:

1. Position the insertion point where you want the table to start (in our case, at the top of the document).
2. From the **Insert** tab, **Tables** group, click the **Table** button. Then drag to create a table with the desired number of columns and rows.

   Note: In this example, a 2-column, 5-row table will be used. Notice that as you drag, a live preview of the table appears in the Word window in the background. When you release the mouse, the table appears and special **Table Tools** appear on the **Ribbon** with **Design** and **Layout** tabs below. **Table Tools** with **Design** and **Layout** tabs below will appear anytime you click inside a table.

(continued on next page)

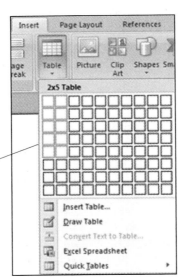

Drag in this table grid to create a table and look at the **Live Preview** on the Word document screen.

Or: From the **Insert** tab, **Tables** group, click the **Table** button, **Insert Table**. The **Insert Table** dialog box appears.

- Type the number of columns you want in the **Number of columns** box; for this example, type **2**.
- Press **TAB** and type the number of rows in the **Number of rows** box; for this example, type **5**.
- Click **OK** to insert the table into your document.

Note: When you click **OK**, the table appears and special **Table Tools** appear on the **Ribbon** with a **Design** tab and **Layout** tab next to each other below **Table Tools**.

Type text inside the cells as desired. Cells will expand automatically to accommodate longer text. If you press **ENTER** by accident, an additional blank line will be added to the cell. Press **BACKSPACE** or click **UNDO** to delete the unwanted line. To move from cell to cell, click the desired cell with the mouse or press **TAB**. To move to the previous cell, press **SHIFT + TAB**. Use the arrow keys to move up or down the rows. To insert an additional row, click in the last cell, and press **TAB**.

(continued on next page)

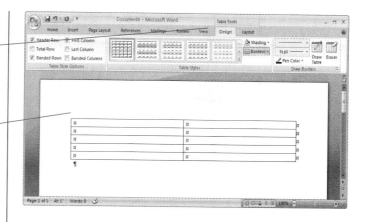

Table Tools appear that include **Design** and **Layout** tabs.

This is a 5x2 table with borders with the insertion point in Cell A1.

If you are in the last cell of a table (Cell B5 in this case), pressing **TAB** would insert an additional row into the table. Click the **Undo** button to remove the unwanted row.

PRACTICE

1. Insert a table with 5 rows and 2 columns, click in Cell A1, and type President.

2. Press **TAB** to move to Cell B1 and type Juanita Cortes-Perin.

3. Press **TAB** (*not* **ENTER**) to move to Cell A2 and continue typing the entries as shown below:

President	Juanita Cortes-Perin
Vice President	Paul J. Anchor
Secretary	Rhetta Jones
Treasurer	Imogene Corker
Faculty Sponsor	Professor Leon South

Your finished table should look like this:

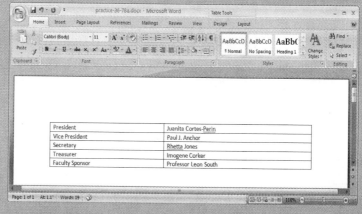

4. Save changes to *practice-36*.

Note: Keep this document open and continue reading.

(continued on next page)

Table—AutoFit to Contents

To resize the width of columns in a table to fit the contents in that table, apply the **AutoFit to Contents** feature.

1. Click anywhere in the table.
2. From **Table Tools, Layout** tab, **Cell Size** group, click the list arrow next to **AutoFit**, and click **AutoFit to Contents**.

   Or: Right-click any table cell, and click **AutoFit, AutoFit to Contents**.
   Or: Select the table (see Lesson 37), and double-click on the right border of any cell.

Note: If any of the lines wrap incorrectly when you use the **AutoFit** feature, point to the cell border to the right of the column that needs adjusting until you see a double-sided arrow and double-click.

The **AutoFit** option will automatically resize the table without changing any other formatting.

3. Note that the table has been resized to accommodate the longest word or words in each column.

PRACTICE *(continued)*

1. Right-click anywhere inside the table.
2. Click **AutoFit, AutoFit to Contents**. Your finished table should look like this:

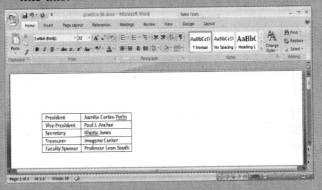

3. Save changes to *practice-36*, and return to GDP.

Go To Textbook

Open Tables With Titles

Table—Merge Cells

Table titles (and subtitles, if used) are typed in the first row of a table. In order to have the title centered over all columns of the table, you must merge the cells in that row to form one cell that extends the entire width of the table.

To merge cells:

1. Select the cells you want to merge.

Site Visitation	September 13-16	Alan C. Wingett
On-Site Interviews	September 14-15	Chad Spencer
Preliminary Decisions	September 23	Sherri Jordan
New York Visits	October 4-7	Pedro Martin
Evaluation Conference	October 8	Sherri Jordan
Final Decision	October 10	Gerald J. Pearson

Merge Cells button

Select cell

Select row

Select column

Select table

Table move handle

Note: To select a cell or row, click the left border of the cell or click just to the left of the row. To select a column, click the top border of the column. To select multiple cells, rows, or columns, drag across and down as desired. The easiest way to select a table is to point to the table until the **table move handle** appears just above the top corner of Cell A1, and then click the **table move handle**.

Or: Under **Table Tools**, click the **Layout** tab. In the **Table** group, click **Select**, and then click **Select Table**.

2. Under **Table Tools**, on the **Layout** tab, in the **Merge** group, click **Merge Cells**. Or right-click over the selected row and click **Merge Cells**. The selected cells are merged into a single cell.

Site Visitation	September 13-16	Alan C. Wingett
On-Site Interviews	September 14-15	Chad Spencer
Preliminary Decisions	September 23	Sherri Jordan
New York Visits	October 4-7	Pedro Martin
Evaluation Conference	October 8	Sherri Jordan
Final Decision	October 10	Gerald J. Pearson

You can use your usual formats (such as center and bold) when formatting the information inside a table.

3. Type the desired information in the merged cell.

(continued on next page)

| VICE PRESIDENTIAL SEARCH SCHEDULE | | |
Harry Wesson Coordinator		
Site Visitation	September 13-16	Alan C. Wingett
On-Site Interviews	September 14-15	Chad Spencer
Preliminary Decisions	September 23	Sherri Jordan
New York Visits	October 4-7	Pedro Martin
Evaluation Conference	October 8	Sherri Jordan
Final Decision	October 10	Gerald J. Pearson

Note: Standard format is to center and type a table title in bold, 14-pt. font and all caps and to insert 1 blank line after the title. Type a subtitle, if used, below the title using upper- and lowercase and bold formatting in a 12-pt. font. Insert 1 blank line after the subtitle rather than after the title if a subtitle is used.

Note: You can merge the cells and then type the title or type the title and then merge the cells. The result is the same.

PRACTICE

1. Select Row 1 in the table shown below.

Row 1

Site Visitation	September 13-16	Alan C. Wingett
On-Site Interviews	September 14-15	Chad Spencer
Preliminary Decisions	September 23	Sherri Jordan
New York Visits	October 4-7	Pedro Martin
Evaluation Conference	October 8	Sherri Jordan
Final Decision	October 10	Gerald J. Pearson

2. Merge the cells.

3. Turn on bold and center alignment, and type the title in all caps in 14-pt. font size: **VICE PRESIDENTIAL SEARCH SCHEDULE**.

4. Press **ENTER**, and type the subtitle Harry Wesson Coordinator in bold, 12-pt. font size.

5. Press **ENTER** 1 time to insert a blank line after the subtitle. Your table should look like this:

| VICE PRESIDENTIAL SEARCH SCHEDULE | | |
Harry Wesson Coordinator		
Site Visitation	September 13-16	Alan C. Wingett
On-Site Interviews	September 14-15	Chad Spencer
Preliminary Decisions	September 23	Sherri Jordan
New York Visits	October 4-7	Pedro Martin
Evaluation Conference	October 8	Sherri Jordan
Final Decision	October 10	Gerald J. Pearson

6. Save changes to *practice-37*.

Note: Keep this document open, and continue reading on the next page.

(continued on next page)

Table—Borders

Borders are the lines that surround each cell in a table. Word applies borders by default when a new table is inserted. When borders are removed, grid lines (light, nonprinting blue dashes) will appear to help you see table cells. You can also apply borders or remove borders from individual cells or from the left, right, top, bottom, and/or inside lines bordering a cell or table.

To remove borders from a table:

1. Select the table or the desired cell(s).
2. From the **Home** tab, **Paragraph** group, click the list arrow next to the **Borders** button, and click the desired border to add it or remove it.

   Note: Be careful to click the list arrow next to the **Borders** button and not the **Borders** button itself. If you click the **Borders** button, the currently displayed border on the button will be applied to the table or selected cell(s).

   Note: The **Borders** button is also available when you click inside the table under **Table Tools**. Click the **Design** tab. In the **Table Styles** group, you will see the **Borders** button.

3. From the drop-down list of borders, click the desired border to add it or click a selected border (shown in orange) to remove it.
4. Repeat this process until the desired borders have been added or removed.

(continued on next page)

Note: If you want to remove all borders at once from a selected table, click **No Border**. If you want to add borders all at once from all cells, click **All Borders**.

Note: If you remove all borders and want to see light blue nonprinting gridlines from a selected table, click **View Gridlines**. The gridlines will appear as in the table below but will not print.

VICE PRESIDENTIAL SEARCH SCHEDULE		
Harry Wesson Coordinator		
Site Visitation	September 13-16	Alan C. Wingett
On-Site Interviews	September 14-15	Chad Spencer
Preliminary Decisions	September 23	Sherri Jordan
New York Visits	October 4-7	Pedro Martin
Evaluation Conference	October 8	Sherri Jordan
Final Decision	October 10	Gerald J. Pearson

To apply (or remove) borders on any side of a cell, such as in a ruled table or resume:

Note: For a ruled table or resume, remove all borders first by following steps 1–4 on the previous page. For a header, follow steps 1–3 below.

1. Click anywhere inside the header area above the first line on a page.
2. From the **Home** tab, **Paragraph** group, click the list arrow next to the **Borders** button, and click the desired border to add it or remove it.
3. Click anywhere outside the header area to close it.

PRACTICE *(continued)*

1. Click inside Cell A1, and automatically adjust the column widths to fit the contents for all columns.
2. Remove borders from this table by following steps 1–4 on page 83. Note the dimmed gridlines that remain.
3. Press **CTRL + F2** to see the **Print Preview**, and observe that borders have been removed and gridlines do not display. Your finished table should look similar to this:

VICE PRESIDENTIAL SEARCH SCHEDULE		
Harry Wesson Coordinator		
Site Visitation	September 13-16	Alan C. Wingett
On-Site Interviews	September 14-15	Chad Spencer
Preliminary Decisions	September 23	Sherri Jordan
New York Visits	October 4-7	Pedro Martin
Evaluation Conference	October 8	Sherri Jordan
Final Decision	October 10	Gerald J. Pearson

4. Click **Close**.
5. Save changes to *practice-37*, and return to GDP.

Go To Textbook

Open Tables With Column Headings

Table—Center Horizontally

When you insert a table, the table extends from margin to margin and is left-aligned by default. However, if you adjust column widths, the table width shrinks and you will need to change the horizontal alignment of the entire table to center.

To change the horizontal alignment of a table:

1. Click inside the table.
2. Under **Table Tools**, on the **Layout** tab, in the **Table** group, click **Properties**; or right-click the table and click **Table Properties**.

Click **Center** to center a table horizontally.

3. Click the alignment option desired (in this case, **Center**).
4. Click **OK**.

Or:

1. Select the table by clicking the table move handle just above the top corner of Cell A1.
2. From the **Home** tab, **Paragraph** group, click the **Center** button.

(continued on next page)

If you click **Center**, the table is centered between the margins, as shown below:

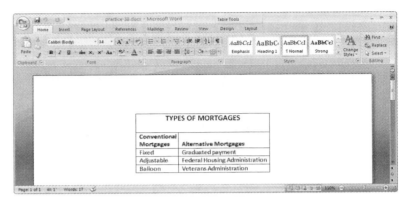

Note: You must be in **Print Layout** view for the table to appear centered.

PRACTICE

1. Select Rows 1 and 2 and bold them. (*Hint*: To select a cell or row, click just to the left of the row.)
2. Delete the space between *Conventional* and *Mortgage*, and press **ENTER** 1 time to create a 2-line column heading.
3. Click in front of *Alternative Mortgages* in Cell B2 and press **ENTER** 1 time to push it down so it will align vertically at the bottom of the cell.
4. Select Row 1 (the blank row), and merge the cells.
5. Click in Row 1 and type the title TYPES OF MORTGAGES centered, in bold, with a 14-pt. font, and press **ENTER** 1 time to insert a blank line below the title. Your table should now look like this:

TYPES OF MORTGAGES	
Conventional Mortgages	Alternative Mortgages
Fixed	Graduated payment
Adjustable	Federal Housing Administration
Balloon	Veterans Administration

(continued on next page)

6. Right-click any table cell, and click **AutoFit, AutoFit to Contents**

TYPES OF MORTGAGES	
Conventional Mortgages	Alternative Mortgages
Fixed	Graduated payment
Adjustable	Federal Housing Administration
Balloon	Veterans Administration

7. Change the horizontal alignment of the table to center. Remember, you must be in **Print Layout** view to be able to see the table centered horizontally.

Note: Keep this document open and continue reading.

Table—Center Page

Use the **Page Setup** command to center text vertically between the top and bottom margins on a page (see the illustration below).

Before vertical centering, the table is too high on the page.

After vertical centering, the table looks centered on the page between the top and bottom margins.

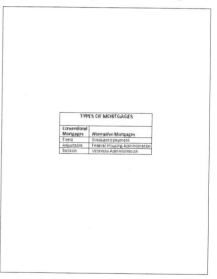

To center text (such as a table) vertically on a page:

1. Position the insertion point anywhere on the page you want centered.
2. From the **Page Layout** tab, click the **Page Setup Dialog Box Launcher**.

(continued on next page)

3. Click the **Layout** tab.

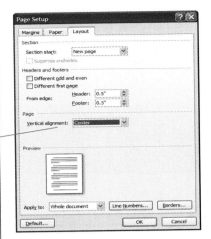

Clicking **Center** will center the text between the top and bottom margins.

4. Click the down arrow in the **Vertical alignment** list box, and click **Center**.

5. Click **OK**.

PRACTICE *(continued)*

1. Center the table vertically on the page.
2. Use **Print Preview** to view the centered table.
3. Save changes to *practice-38*, and return to GDP.

 Textbook

Ruled Tables With Number Columns

Table—Align Text in a Column

Keyboard shortcut reminder:
Left = **CTRL + L**
Center = **CTRL + E**
Right = **CTRL + R**
Justified = **CTRL + J**

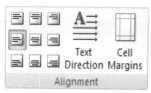

Alignment group

You can improve the readability and appearance of a table by changing the column alignment.

To align text in columns:

1. Select the cells or text to format.
2. Under **Table Tools**, on the **Layout** tab, in the **Alignment** group, click the **Align Top Left, Align Top Center,** or **Align Top Right** button.

   Or: From the **Home** tab, **Paragraph** group, click the **Align Text Left**, **Center**, **Align Text Right**, or **Justify** button.
   Or: On the keyboard, use one of the keyboard shortcuts.
   Or: Right-click the selected area, click **Cell Alignment**, and click the desired choice.

PRACTICE

1. Select Rows 1 and 2 and bold them.
2. Select Columns B, C, and D, and align all items at the right.
3. Delete the space between *Vehicle* and *Category*, and press **ENTER** 1 time to create a 2-line column heading.
4. Click in front of each of the 1-line column headings in Cells B2, C2, and D2; and press **ENTER** 1 time to push them down so they will align vertically at the bottom of their cells.
5. Select Row 1 (the blank row), and merge the cells.
6. Click in Row 1 and type the title PRICE COMPARISONS centered, in bold, with a 14-pt. font, and press **ENTER** 1 time.
7. Change to 12-pt. font, type the subtitle New Cars, and press **ENTER** 1 time to insert a blank line below the subtitle.
8. Right-click any table cell, and click **AutoFit, AutoFit to Contents**

PRICE COMPARISONS New Cars			
Vehicle Category	AutoMart	SmartBuy	Dealer
Sedan	$20,861	$21,216	$23,743
SUV	28,700	29,562	32,270
Truck	18,600	20,247	21,983

(continued on next page)

9. Center the table horizontally; select the table with the **table move handle**; and from the **Home** tab, **Paragraph** group, click the **Center** button.
10. Remove all borders from the table; select the table; from the **Home** tab, **Paragraph** group, click the list arrow next to the **Borders** button, and click the **No Border** button.
11. Select Row 2; from the **Home** tab, **Paragraph** group, click the list arrow next to the **Borders** button, and click the **Top Border** and then click the **Bottom Border** buttons to apply borders to the top and bottom of Row 2.
12. Select Row 5; from the **Home** tab, **Paragraph** group, click the list arrow next to the **Borders** button, and click the **Bottom Border** button to apply a border to the bottom of Row 5.

   Note: Because the bottom border was just used, you can click the **Bottom Border** button directly without having to click the list arrow.

13. Center the table vertically. From the **Page Layout** tab, click the **Page Setup Dialog Box Launcher**. From the **Layout** tab, under **Page**, click **Vertical alignment**, **Center**, **OK**.
14. Your table should now look like this in **Print Preview:**

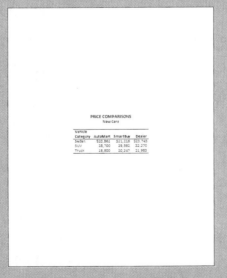

Go To Textbook

15. Save changes to *practice-39*, and return to GDP.

Left-Bound Business Reports With Footnotes

Margins

Margins represent the distance (blank space) between the edge of the paper and the text. Word's default margins are 1 inch all around. If you change margins, the new settings affect the entire document, not just the current page. Left-bound reports use a 1.5-inch left margin.

Note: Display the ruler before setting margins. To display the ruler, click the **View Ruler** button located above the vertical scroll bars. Click it again to hide it.

1. From the **Page Layout** tab, **Page Setup** group, click **Margins**, **Custom Margins**. The **Page Setup** window appears.

Type **1.5** in the **Left** box to set the left margin for a left-bound report.

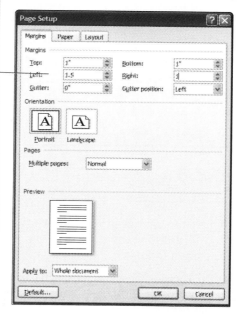

(continued on next page)

2. From the **Margins** tab, click in the **Left** box, and type **1.5** or click the arrows to increase or decrease margins as desired.
3. Click in any of the other **Margins** boxes as desired to change margin settings.
4. Click **OK**.

PRACTICE

1. Note the line endings in each line *before* margins are changed.
2. Note the ruler indicates a 6.5-inch line of writing.

Before margin are changed, the ruler indicates a 6.5-inch line of writing, which is the default setting for 1-inch side margins.

and those workers who initially resisted the technology declare it is easy to learn and has

enabled them to compete with any business that has previously published such documents as

reports, newsletters, and company brochures." The cost of laying out a page has now been cut

3. Change the left margin to 1.5 inch.
4. Note the line endings in each line *after* margins are changed.
5. Note the ruler indicates a 6-inch line of writing.

After the left margin is changed, the ruler indicates a 6-inch line of writing with a 1.5-inch left margin and a 1-inch right margin, which are the margins for a left-bound report.

and those workers who initially resisted the technology declare it is easy to learn and

has enabled them to compete with any business that has previously published such

documents as reports, newsletters, and company brochures." The cost of laying out a

6. Save the changes to *practice-41*.

Note: Keep this document open and continue reading.

Footnotes

Inserting footnotes is easy because Word automatically numbers, positions, and formats the footnotes for you.

To insert a footnote:

1. In **Print Layout** view, click **directly after** the character where you want to insert the footnote number (a superscript with a sequential footnote number).

   Note: Do **not** type the footnote number either in the document or in the footnote itself. It will appear in both places automatically in the next step. Do **not** insert a space between the last character in the text and the footnote number.

(continued on next page)

Position the insertion point exactly where you want the foot-note reference mark to appear.

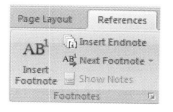

Footnotes group with **Insert Footnote** button

Word formats footnotes in a smaller font size than normal text.

1. From the **References** tab, in the **Footnotes** group, click **Insert Footnote**.

Or: On the keyboard, press **CTRL + ALT + F**.

Note: If you want to use the **Footnote and Endnote** dialog box, from the **References** tab, click the **Footnotes Dialog Box Launcher**.

2. Type the footnote entry at the bottom of the page.

Note: Immediately, a footnote number appears automatically in the text, and then the insertion point moves automatically to the bottom of the page, where a divider line and a footnote number also appear. Word will automatically adjust footnote numbers when entries are added or deleted. Note that the font size for the footnote entry is smaller than normal. Do **not** add or remove the space after the foot-note—just begin typing the footnote where the insertion point appears. Do **not** press **ENTER** after typing the footnote. Use italic to type titles of major works such as book and magazine titles.

3. Move back inside the main text and click where you want your next footnote number to appear.

4. Repeat steps 1, 2, and 3 for each additional footnote.

[1] Louise Plachta and Leonard E. Flannery, *The Desktop Publishing Revolution, 2d ed.,* Computer Publications, Inc., Los Angeles, 2005, pp. 568-569.
[2] Terry Denton, "Newspaper Cuts Costs, Increases Quality," *The Monthly Press,* October 2005, p. 160.

(continued on next page)

> has enabled them to compete with any business that has previously published such
>
> documents as reports, newsletters, and company brochures."[1] The cost of laying out a
>
> ~~page has now been cut considerably with this revolutionary technology.~~[2] It is no
>
> wonder, then, that companies worldwide are overly enthusiastic about hiring trained

Footnote superscript numbers appear automatically in the text at the point where you insert them.

To edit a footnote:

1. Click inside the footnote entry.
2. Make any desired changes.

To delete a footnote:

1. Select the footnote number in the document (not in the footnote entry at the bottom of the page).
2. Press **DELETE**.

PRACTICE

1. Click immediately after the ending quotation mark in the first sentence and insert the footnote shown below: **Reminder:** Do **not** type the footnote number. Word inserts the footnote number for you.

   [1] Louise Plachta and Leonard E. Flannery, *The Desktop Publishing Revolution*, 2d ed., Computer Publications, Inc., Los Angeles, 2005, pp. 568-569.

2. Click immediately after the period in the second sentence in the body of the document and insert the following footnote:

   [2] Terry Denton, "Newspaper Cuts Costs, Increases Quality," *The Monthly Press*, October 2005, p. 160.

(continued on next page)

3. Edit Footnote 1 by changing the page references to pp. 558–559.

4. Use the **Print Preview** to view your document; it should look similar to the following report page:

2

and those workers who initially resisted the technology declare it is easy to learn and

has enabled them to compete with any business that has previously published such

documents as reports, newsletters, and company brochures."³ The cost of laying out a

page has now been cut considerably with this revolutionary technology.⁴ It is no

wonder, then, that companies worldwide are overly enthusiastic about hiring trained

personnel with these skills.

³ Louise Plachta and Leonard E. Flannery, *The Desktop Publishing Revolution*, 2d ed., Computer Publications, Inc., Los Angeles, 2009, pp. 568–569.

⁴ Terry Denton, "Newspaper Cuts Costs, Increases Quality," *The Monthly Press*, October 2009, p. 160.

Note that the footnote references are positioned at the bottom of a page regardless of how much text is on the page. Note the wider 1.5-inch left margin.

 Textbook

5. Save the changes to *practice-41*, and return to GDP.

Reports in APA Style

Headers and Footers

Header button

Footer button

A *header* is text that is positioned inside the top margin and can be set to appear on every page in a document. A *footer* is text that is positioned inside the bottom margin and can also be set to appear on every page. The header or footer can be as simple as a page number or as complex as text plus lines and graphics.

To insert a header into every page of a document:

1. From the first page of your document, from the **Insert** tab, **Header & Footer** group, click **Header, Blank**.

   Note: You will see [Type text], a placeholder reminder that will disappear when you type text in the header.

2. Type any desired text at the left margin or press **TAB** once to move to the center and again to move to the right margin, typing any desired text as you go.

3. Move the insertion point to the desired position in the header, and then add the automatic page number by doing this: from the **Design** tab, **Header & Footer** group, click **Page Number**, **Current Position**, **Plain Number**.

   Note: If the wrong page number is displayed or if you want to set the page number to start at a different number, do this: from the **Insert** tab, in the **Header & Footer** group, click **Page Number**. Click **Format Page Numbers**. In the **Start at** box, type the desired number; click **OK.**

4. To italicize the header or make any font changes, press **CTRL + A** to select all text; then make any desired font changes.

5. Press the right arrow on the keyboard to deselect the text and to move to the line below the header.

6. To add a bottom border, from the **Home** tab, **Paragraph** group, click the list arrow on the **Borders** button, and click the **Bottom Border** button.

(continued on next page)

Normally, Word displays the same header and footer on all pages. Sometimes, you may not want a header or footer to appear on the first page.

To hide the header on the first page:

Note: Before you begin the steps below, do this: From the **Page Layout** tab, click the **Page Setup Dialog Box Launcher,** and then click the **Layout** tab. Under **Headers and Footers,** verify that **Different first page** is *unchecked;* click **OK.**

1. Follow steps 1-6 in the preceding section, and skip any that do not apply to the header you want.
2. When your header is finished and while the header is still open, from the **Design** tab, **Options** group, click **Different First Page**.

Note: You should now be in the **First Page Header** section and it should be blank. If the page number is still in the **First Page Header**, select the page number and cut it.

3. Scroll down to the second page to see the header, which should now have text, the page number, and a bottom border.

To insert a footer into every page of a document:

1. From the **Insert** tab, **Header & Footer** group, click **Footer, Blank**.

Note: You will see [Type text], a placeholder reminder that will disappear when you type text in the footer.

2. Type any desired text at the left margin or press **TAB** once to move to the center, and again to move to the right margin, typing any desired text as you go.
3. To add an automatic page number, the insertion point should be in the desired position in the footer; from the **Design** tab, **Header & Footer** group, click **Page Number**, **Current Position**, **Plain Number**.

Note: If the wrong page number is displayed or if you want to set the page number to start at a different number, do this: from the **Insert** tab, in the **Header & Footer** group, click **Page Number**. Click **Format Page Numbers**. In the **Start at** box, type the desired number; click **OK.**

4. To italicize the footer or make any font changes, press **CTRL + A** to select all text; then make any desired font changes.

To close a header or footer, double-click anywhere inside the document area to close the pane and to return to the document. (The header and/or footer should now be dimmed and the document should be active.)

To edit a header or footer, double-click anywhere inside the header or footer area. (The document should now be dimmed and the header or footer should be active.)

To remove a header or footer, from the **Insert** tab, **Header & Footer** group, click **Footer, Remove Footer**, or click **Header, Remove Header**.

(continued on next page)

Note: If you create a new document and insert a header to display on page 2 of the document, the header text may seem to disappear. The text is not lost, but will display when the document text is two pages in length. You may want to insert headers and footers after you finish typing the document.

PRACTICE

1. Type the title `Toll-Free Telephone Service` at the top of the first page.
2. Press **ENTER** 1 time, type `Michael Dear` as the byline, and press **ENTER** again. Center the title and byline.
3. Press **ENTER** twice at the end of the first sentence, press **TAB** to indent the paragraph, and then click the up arrow to move up one line, and type `Analysis of Costs and Benefits` as a centered main heading. Delete the extra space after the period at the end of the first paragraph.
4. Press **ENTER** at the end of the third paragraph in the Analysis of Costs and Benefits section, and type `SmartToll Benefits` as a subheading at the left margin in italic.
5. Press **ENTER** at the end of the next paragraph in the Analysis of Costs and Benefits section, and type `SmartToll Fees` as a subheading at the left margin in italic.
6. Add a right-aligned header to the report with text and a page number that starts at 3. From the **Insert** tab, **Header & Footer** group, click **Header, Blank**.
7. Press **TAB** twice to move to the right margin.
8. Type `Telephone Service`, and press the **SPACE BAR** once.
9. From the **Design** tab, **Header & Footer** group, click **Page Number**, **Current Position**, **Plain Number**.
10. From the **Insert** tab, in the **Header & Footer** group, click **Page Number**. Click **Format Page Numbers**. In the **Start at** box, type 3; click **OK.**

(continued on next page)

11. Click inside the document area to close the header. Your document should look similar to this:

Telephone Service 3

Toll-Free Telephone Service

Michael Dear

In order to determine the feasibility of providing a toll-free telephone service to United Manufacturing domestic spare-parts customers, the management team evaluated the costs and benefits.

Analysis of Costs and Benefits

Incoming telephone call time usage was recorded the week of November 12-17, 409 domestic customers were surveyed in October/November, and a telephone interview was conducted with a phone company toll-free representative in October. The criteria used were the costs and benefits of a toll-free service, the value customers place on a toll-free service, and how to communicate a toll-free service.

United Manufacturing currently uses Digital Connect as their long-distance telephone carrier. The required toll-free telephone service and cost analysis are based on information from, and a telephone interview with Digital Connect.

According to Art Neumann, a Digital Connect Long-Distance Network Sales Specialist, the service recommended for United Manufacturing is SmartToll. SmartToll is an inward toll-free service that utilizes the existing telephone lines to receive the 800-number calls.

SmartToll Benefits

The advantage of this service is all of the existing lines currently used to place and receive calls are available to receive the incoming 800-number calls. Because the SmartToll service distributes the incoming calls among the available lines, there is a reduction in the chance a caller will receive a busy signal. Several customers indicated in the comment section

Telephone Service 4

of the questionnaire that if United Manufacturing were to offer an 800 number, they should include sufficient service to handle the expected volume of incoming calls.

SmartToll Fees

At no additional charge, SmartToll service allows the customer to redirect a call destination over the Internet. The customer is provided with an individual Web interface. This allows the customer the flexibility to take toll-free calls on any office, home or cell phone. The customer can control where the toll-free number rings with just a click. No additional phone lines are needed. Flat rate pricing in state or out-of-state is available.

Go To **Textbook**

12. Save the changes to *practice-42*, and return to GDP.

Report Citations

Hanging Indent

A paragraph formatted with a hanging indent displays with the first line at the left margin and carryover lines indented 0.5 inch. The list of sources in bibliographies, reference lists, and Works Cited pages are all formatted with hanging indents.

To format a hanging indent:

1. Position the insertion point where you want to begin indenting (or select the text you want indented).
2. From the **Home** tab, click the **Paragraph Dialog Box Launcher.**
3. From the **Paragraph** window, click the **Indents and Spacing** tab.
4. In the **Special** box, click the down arrow and click **Hanging**; then click **OK**.

   Or: On the keyboard, press **CTRL + T**.

Note: If you have already typed the document and want to apply a hanging indent, select the desired text first before applying a hanging indent.

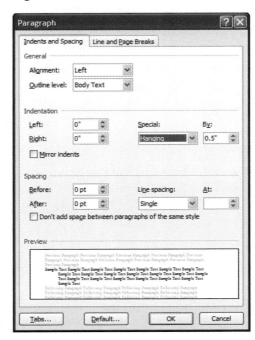

(continued on next page)

---

5. Begin typing the first reference. The first line will begin at the left margin. At the end of a line, the text will automatically wrap to the next line and start at the indent.

6. Press **ENTER** once or twice as appropriate and type the next reference.

To end a hanging indent:

1. When you finish typing the hanging-indented text, press **ENTER.**

2. From the **Home** tab, click the **Paragraph Dialog Box Launcher.** From the **Paragraph** window, click the **Indents and Spacing** tab.

3. In the **Special** box, click the down arrow and click **(none).** Then click **OK.**

Or: On the keyboard, press **CTRL + SHIFT + T** to return the insertion point to the left margin for all lines.

If you display the **Ruler** in Word, it is easier to verify that a hanging indent has been correctly set. To display the **Ruler,** click the **View Ruler** button at the top of the vertical scroll area. To hide the **Ruler,** click the **View Ruler** button again.

Note that the hanging indent marker on the ruler moves over 0.5 inch to the right when you format a paragraph with a hanging indent.

Hanging indent marker

Hanging indent applied

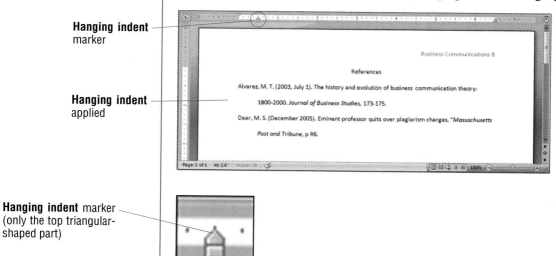

Hanging indent marker (only the top triangular-shaped part)

(continued on next page)

PRACTICE

Note: This practice exercise is formatted as a reference list page in APA format. See the Reference Manual in the front of this book or in GDP for bibliography format for business or academic style and Works Cited pages in MLA style.

1. Select the two reference citations and format them with a hanging indent.
2. Click at the end of the second reference, press **ENTER** 1 time, and type this third reference citation with a hanging indent.

   ```
   Felix, E. A., & Connor, E. (2002). A guide to
   first-class writing in today's world. New York:
   New York Press.
   ```

   Your document should look similar to this:

   Business Communications 8

   References

   Alvarez, M. T. (2003, July 1). The history and evolution of business communication theory:

   1800-2000. *Journal of Business Studies*, 173-175.

   Dear, M. S. (December 2005). Eminent professor quits over plagiarism charges, "*Massachusetts*

   Post and Tribune, p R6.

   Felix, E. A., & Connor, E. (2002). *A guide to first-class writing in today's world*. New York: New

   York Press.

Textbook

3. Save changes to *practice-44*, and return to GDP.

Preliminary Report Pages

Tab Set—Dot Leaders

Word has default tab stops set every 0.5 inch starting at the left margin. When you press **TAB** in a document to indent a paragraph, these default tab settings are the reason you move in by 0.5 inch. You can see them on the ruler as tick marks every 0.5 inch.

Note: To display the horizontal and vertical rulers, click the **View Ruler** button at the top of the vertical scroll area. To hide the rulers, click the **View Ruler** button again.

0.5-inch default tab
stop marks

You can set custom tabs in any location as needed. For example, for a table of contents, you will need to set a 0.5-inch left tab and a 6.5-inch right dot leader tab as shown below. In this lesson, you will set tabs by using the menu.

When custom tabs are set, all default 0.5-inch tabs are deleted to the left of the new custom tabs, and the tick marks are therefore removed. A table of contents requires a 0.5-inch left tab to indent the subsections of a report and a 6.5-inch right dot leader tab. When you type a major heading and press **TAB**, the dot leader tab you move to fills the space between the heading and the page number with consecutive periods (called *dot leaders*) to lead the reader's eye across the page to the page number. When you type a minor heading, you will press **TAB** to indent the subheading by 0.5 inch, and press **TAB** again to insert the dot leaders.

0.5-inch left tab marker

6.5-inch right tab marker
for dot leaders

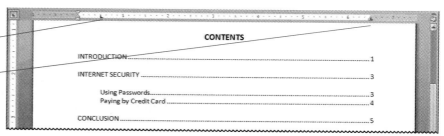

(continued on next page)

To set a custom tab using the menu:

1. Position the insertion point on the line where you want the new tab to start (or select the paragraphs where you want to change the tabs).
2. From the **Home** or **Page Layout** tab, click the **Paragraph Dialog Box Launcher.**
3. From the **Paragraph** window, click the **Indents and Spacing** tab, and click the **Tabs** button. The **Tabs** dialog box appears.

Type the position of each tab setting in the **Tab stop position** box, and click **Set** after each one.

Click the desired **Alignment** button.

Click the desired **Leader** option. Click **2** for dot leaders.

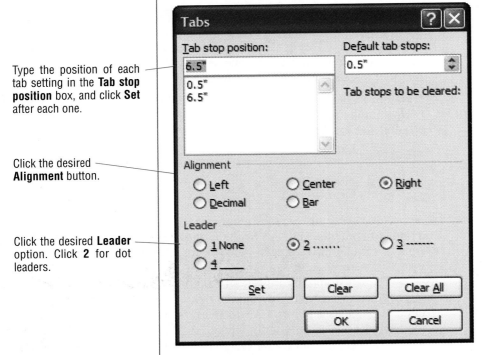

4. In the **Tab stop position** box, type the position of the tab you want set.
5. In the **Alignment** section, click the desired alignment. (You would typically set a right tab for dot leaders.)
6. In the **Leader** section, click **2.**
7. Click **Set.**

   Note: You can change from a dot-leader tab to hyphens or an underline by clicking **3** or **4**.
   Note: When you set a custom tab, default tabs to the left of the new setting will be deleted. Therefore, if you are typing a table of contents with subheadings, you should also set a left tab at 0.5 inch. (*Hint:* Type **.5** in the **Tab stop position** box, click **Left** in the **Alignment** section, and click **None** in the **Leader** section.)

8. Click **OK.**

(continued on next page)

PRACTICE

1. Set a left tab at 0.5 inch and a right dot-leader tab at 6.5 inches.
2. Press **ENTER** 5 times.
3. Type CONTENTS centered in bold with a 14-pt. font size.
4. Press **ENTER** 2 times.
5. Type the following text as shown with a 12-pt. font size:

```
INTRODUCTION  ...................1
INTERNET SECURITY ...............3
   Using Passwords  ..............3
   Paying by Credit Card  ........4
CONCLUSION  .....................5
```

    Your document should look similar to this:

CONTENTS

INTRODUCTION... 1

INTERNET SECURITY 3

      Using Passwords 3
      Paying by Credit Card 4

CONCLUSION.. 5

Go To **Textbook**

6. Save changes to *practice-45*, and return to GDP.

Letters in Modified-Block Style

Ruler Tabs

You can use the horizontal ruler to set tab stops and indents for selected paragraphs.

To display the horizontal and vertical rulers, click the **View Ruler** button at the top of the vertical scroll area. To hide the rulers, click the **View Ruler** button again.

Tab Set

Word enables you to set left tabs, center tabs, right tabs, and decimal tabs at different positions. Default tabs are displayed on the horizontal ruler as tick marks. Custom tabs are displayed according to type.

The four different kinds of tabs are illustrated below:

Tab selector —

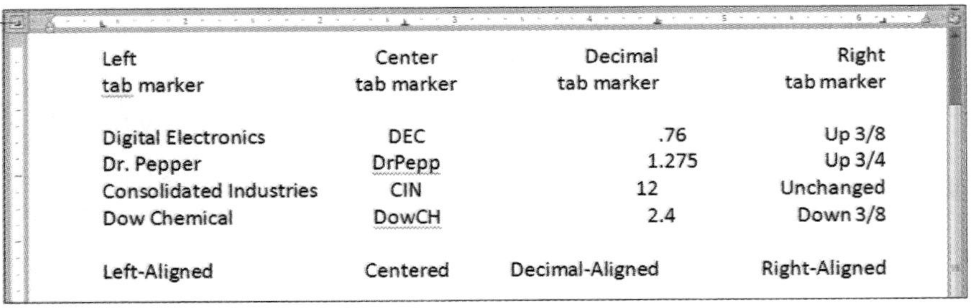

Left tab marker	Center tab marker	Decimal tab marker	Right tab marker
Digital Electronics	DEC	.76	Up 3/8
Dr. Pepper	DrPepp	1.275	Up 3/4
Consolidated Industries	CIN	12	Unchanged
Dow Chemical	DowCH	2.4	Down 3/8
Left-Aligned	Centered	Decimal-Aligned	Right-Aligned

(continued on next page)

When you set a custom tab, Word clears (deletes) all of the default 0.5-inch tab stops to the left of your custom tab. This allows you to go directly to the new tab stop when you press **TAB**. If you need any additional tabs, you will need to set them manually.

To set a custom tab using the ruler:

Left Tab

Center Tab

Right Tab

Decimal Tab

1. Position the insertion point on the line where you want the new tab to start (or select the paragraphs where you want to change the tabs).
2. Click the **Tab Selection** button on the ruler until the appropriate tab marker is displayed.
3. On the ruler, click where you want the new tab to appear.

Click the **Tab Selection** button to select the type of tab.

Then click the ruler.

To clear or move a tab:

1. Position the insertion point on the line where you want the tab change to take effect (or select the paragraphs where you want to change the tabs).
2. To clear (delete) a tab, drag the tab marker off the ruler. To move a tab, drag the tab marker left or right.

To set a tab to position the date, the complimentary closing, and the writer's identification in a modified-block style letter:

1. Set a left tab at 3.25 inches on the ruler.

   Note: If the letter has already been typed, select all lines in the letter before setting the left tab.

2. Click in front of the date in the letter, and press **TAB** 1 time so that the date begins at the 3.25-inch tab.
3. Click in front of the complimentary closing and writer's identification lines and press **TAB** 1 time to begin these lines at the 3.25-inch tab.

(continued on next page)

PRACTICE

Format this letter in modified-block style as follows:

1. Select all lines of the letter, and set a left tab at 3.25 inches on the ruler.

2. Click in front of the date, complimentary closing, and writer's identification, and press **TAB** 1 time to begin these lines at 3.25 inches.

If you click the **Show/Hide** button to view formatting marks, your screen should look similar to the one below. The black arrows indicate where you have pressed **TAB**.

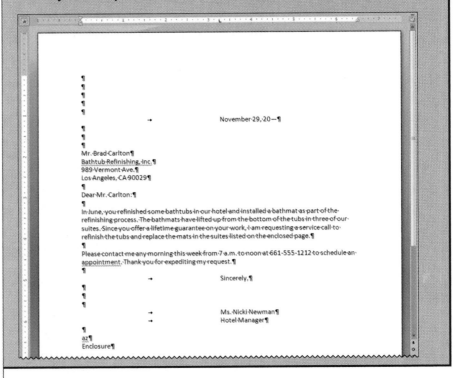

(continued on next page)

3. Move the insertion point to the blank line below the enclosure notation, and insert a manual page break. (*Hint*: press **CTRL+ENTER**.)

4. Clear the left tab from the second page.

5. Set a left tab at 1.5 inches on the ruler and a right tab at 4.5 inches on the ruler.

6. Type the following lines, remembering to press **TAB** 1 time before each building name and 1 time before each suite name.

```
Building A      Grande Suite
Building C      Presidential Suite
Building F      Del Mar Suite
```

When you're finished with the second page, your screen should look similar to the following:

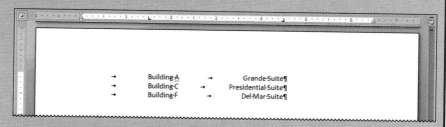

Textbook

7. Save the changes to *practice-50*, and return to GDP.

Traditional Resumes

Fonts

The term *font* refers to the general shape of a character. There are two types of fonts—serif and sans serif. A *serif font* has short lines extending from the edges of letters. A *sans serif font* does not have these lines. The default font in Word is Calibri, a sans serif font. Shown below are some examples of different fonts you can use.

Serif fonts
Cambria
Times New Roman

Sans serif fonts
Calibri
Arial

You can easily change the font in the text of your document. Avoid, however, using too many different fonts in the same document. In a resume, you will use Cambria for the heading information in the first row.

To change fonts:

1. Position the insertion point where you want to begin using the new font (or select the text you want to change).
2. From the **Home** tab, **Font** group, click the down arrow to the right of the **Font** box.
3. Click the desired font (scroll down the list if necessary).

Or: From the **Home** tab, **Font** group, click the **Font Dialog Box Launcher**.
Or: On the keyboard, press **CTRL + D**.

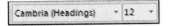

Font box

(continued on next page)

Click the **Font** tab if necessary. When the **Font** dialog box appears, click the font you want; then click **OK**.

You can also change fonts (as well as other text attributes) through the **Font** dialog box.

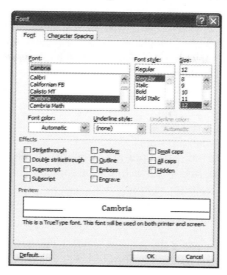

Note: As you begin choosing fonts, notice that each choice is added to the font drop-down list under **Recently Used Fonts** with the most recently used ones first.

PRACTICE

1. In Row 1, select ANGELICA P. JUAREZ, center the name, and change the font to Cambria Bold 14 pt.
2. Select the two lines below the name, center them, and change the font to Cambria Bold 12 pt. Your document should look similar to this.

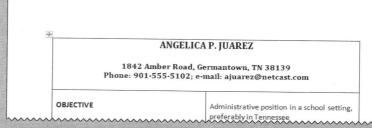

3. Save changes to *practice-51*.

Note: Keep this document open, and continue reading on the next page.

(continued on next page)

Table—Change Column Width

There are several ways to change table column width. In Lesson 36, you learned to use the **AutoFit to Contents** feature. This lesson will show you how to change the column width using the mouse and the **Table Properties** dialog box.

To change table column width using the mouse:

◀‖▶

Resize pointer

1. Display the horizontal ruler by clicking the **View Ruler** button.
2. Point to the right border of the table column until the mouse changes to a resize pointer.
3. With the resize pointer showing, click and hold the mouse button; note the dotted vertical line that appears along the full length of the border extending up to the ruler.
4. Drag the column border until the dotted vertical line points to the desired position on the ruler above.

Note: As long as the cell is not selected, dragging the right border adjusts the entire column width, not just the cell width. Hold down **ALT** as you drag to see the exact ruler measurements. Double-click the right border of a column to adjust the width of the column to the widest cell entry.

To change table column width using the **Table Properties** dialog box:

1. Select the column or click in the column.
2. Right-click, and click **Table Properties**.
3. Click the **Column** tab in the **Table Properties** dialog box.
4. In the size area, check **Preferred width**, and type the desired width in the **Preferred width** box.
5. Click **OK**.

(continued on next page)

PRACTICE *(continued)*

1. Display the ruler, and point to the right border of Column A until the mouse pointer changes to a resize pointer.
2. Double-click the right border to adjust the width of the column to the widest entry.
3. Point to the right border of Column B until the mouse pointer changes to a resize pointer, and drag the column border to the right until the border is positioned at about 6.5 inches on the ruler. If you prefer, you can also double-click the border to position it at 6.5 inches on the ruler.
4. Press **CRTL + HOME** to move to the top of the document, and press **ENTER** 5 times.
5. With **Show/Hide** on, select the 5 blank lines you just inserted, and change the font to Calibri (Body) 12 pt.
6. Click in Row 1, remove all borders from the table, and apply a bottom border to Row 1. (*Hint:* Select the table. From the **Home** tab, **Paragraph** group, click the list arrow next to the **Borders** button, and click **No Border.** Select Row 1, and click the **Bottom Border** button.)
7. Click the **Print Preview** button. Compare your document in **Print Preview** and in **Print Layout** view. Your document should look similar to this.

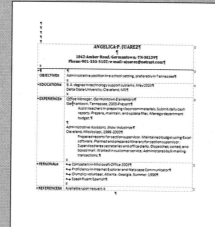

Print Layout view   **Print Preview** view

Go To Textbook

8. Save changes to *practice-51*, and return to GDP.

Electronic Resumes

Saving in Text-Only Format

If you want to send a resume electronically via e-mail, you must save it in a format that is readable by a variety of computers (PC, Macintosh, etc.) and compatible with a variety of software so that your resume will have the best chance of being viewed at its final destination. When you save a Word file as a plain text file (*.txt), it will contain only unformatted text. Formatting, pictures, and so forth, will not be stored.

To save a document as a plain text file:

1. With the desired document open, press **CTRL + A** to select the entire document, and change the font to Courier New 10 pt.
2. Click the **Microsoft Office Button**, and click **Save As**.
3. When the **Save As** dialog box appears, click the arrow next to the **Save in** box to browse to the desired directory to save the file.
4. Type a file name in the **File name** box.
5. Click the arrow next to the **File name** box, scroll down the list, click **Plain Text (*.txt),** and click **Save**.

Note: If a **File Conversion** dialog box opens with warnings and a preview, click **OK**.

Click **Plain Text (*.txt)** to save in text-only format.

PRACTICE

1. With the desired document open, press **CTRL + A** to select the entire document, and change the font to Courier New 10 pt.

Note: If you reopen a file previously saved as **Plain Text (*.txt)**, the font will automatically change to **10.5** and the left and right margins will

(continued on next page)

---

change to **1.04**. This is a style change controlled by Word 2007. Modifying styles is an advanced Word feature that is beyond the scope of this manual. The slight change in font size and margins will not affect the overall appearance of the document.

2. Click the **Microsoft Office Button**, and click **Save As**.

3. Save this file with the same file name *practice-52* but with the **Plain Text** file format.

4. Click **Save**.

5. Click **OK** if a **File Conversion** dialog box appears.

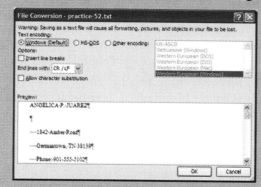

Your file should look similar to this:

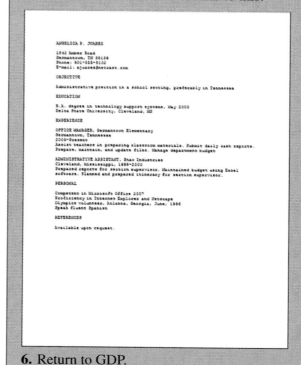

Textbook

6. Return to GDP.

Agendas and Minutes of Meetings

Hyphenation

Hyphenation reduces the ragged appearance of unjustified text because it divides words as needed at the end of a line rather than moving the entire word to the next line. Hyphenation also reduces the amount of blank space inserted between words and letters in justified text.

To hyphenate words automatically:

Hyphenation button

1. From the **Page Layout** tab, in the **Page Setup** group, click the **Hyphenation** button, **Hyphenation Options**. . . .
2. In the **Hyphenation** dialog box, check **Automatically hyphenate document** if it is not already checked.

Note: Word has automatic hyphenation unchecked (turned off) by default. Even if you turn automatic hyphenation on by checking **Automatically hyphenate document**, the default for the next new document you create in Word (either inside or outside of GDP) will have automatic hyphenation unchecked (turned off).

Check **Automatically hyphenate document** and set **Limit consecutive hyphens** to **2**.

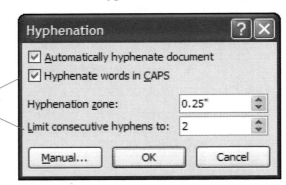

3. In the **Limit consecutive hyphens to:** box, click the up arrow until you see **2**.
4. Click **OK**.

The hyphens Word inserts in words are called *soft hyphens* because they are inserted only when needed. If, during editing, a hyphenated word moves to the middle of the line, Word automatically removes the hyphen.

(continued on next page)

PRACTICE

1. From the **Page Layout** tab, in the **Page Setup** group, click **Hyphenation**, **Hyphenation Options**. Make sure that **Automatically hyphenate document** is *unchecked*; click **OK**.
2. Note that no words are divided in Column B. Your document should look similar to the one below.

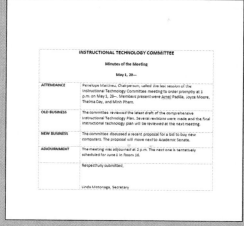

Hyphenation off

3. From the **Page Layout** tab, in the **Page Setup** group, click **Hyphenation**, **Hyphenation Options**. Make sure that **Automatically hyphenate document** *is* checked; click **OK**.
4. Note that several words are divided in Column B. Your document should look similar to the one below:

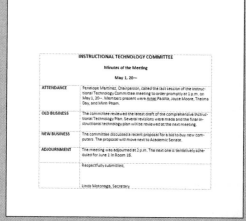

Hyphenation on

5. Save changes to *practice-67*, and return to GDP.

Reports Formatted in Columns

Columns

You can prepare a document in newspaper-style columns or add columns to any part of your document. Text flows from the bottom of one column to the top of the next column. You must be in **Print Layout** view in order to view the columns on the screen.

To add columns to a document:

1. In **Print Layout** view, position the insertion point where you want the columns to begin, and select the text to appear in columns.
2. From the **Page Layout** tab, in the **Page Setup** group, click **Columns.**
3. Then click **One**, **Two**, **Three**, etc., for the desired number of columns.

   Or: Click **More Columns**; the **Columns** dialog box appears.

In newspaper-style columns, text flows from the bottom of one column to the top of the next.

Type the number of desired columns or click the desired **Presets** box.

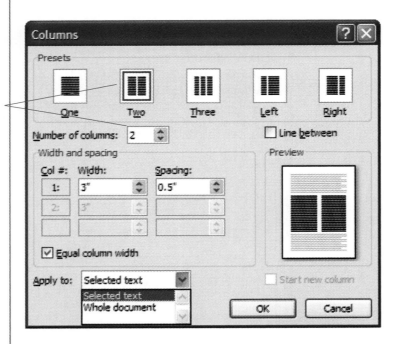

4. Click the desired **Presets** box or type the desired number of columns in the **Number of columns** box.

(continued on next page)

---

5. If you have selected text, click **Selected text** in the **Apply to** box.

   Or: If you have not selected text, and you want the columns to apply to the whole document, click **Whole document** in the **Apply to** box. If you want the columns to begin at the insertion point, click **This point forward** in the **Apply to** box.

   As you're typing, when you reach the bottom of one column, the insertion point automatically moves to the top of the next column. Sometimes, however, you may want to force a column to break at a certain point. Or you may want to have the text distributed equally among the columns to balance the text across the page.

   To insert a column break:

1. Position the insertion point where you want to start the new column.
2. Press **CTRL+SHIFT+ENTER**.

   To balance the columns:

1. Position the insertion point at the end of the text you want to balance.
2. From the **Page Layout** tab, in the **Page Setup** group, click the **Breaks** button. A list of **Page Breaks** and **Section Breaks** appears.

Breaks button

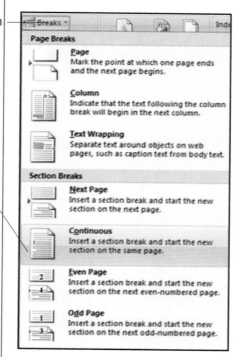

Click **Continuous** to balance the columns so the text is evenly distributed among the columns.

3. Click **Continuous**; then click **OK**.
   The text is then evenly divided among all the columns.

(continued on next page)

Unbalanced column

Balanced columns

Note: Go to Lesson 42, Headers and Footers, and review the steps to hide the header on the first page of a document so that you will be prepared to format the headers in the reports in Lesson 69.

PRACTICE

1. Turn **Show/Hide** on. Select the second paragraph and format it in two columns.
2. Select the third paragraph and format it in three columns.
3. Position the insertion point at the end of the third paragraph and balance the columns. Your screen should now look like this:

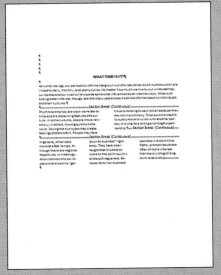

Go To   **Textbook**

4. Save the changes to *practice-69*, and return to GDP.

Special Letter Features

Sort

You can sort text alphabetically, numerically, or by date in ascending (A to Z, zero to nine, etc.) or descending (Z to A, etc.) order.

To perform a sort:

1. Select only the paragraphs to be sorted. In this example, you would select the bulleted list.

Sort button

- System clock
- Data rate
- Bandwidth
- Bus width

2. From the **Home** tab, in the **Paragraph** group, click the **Sort** button.

Note: Information in tables may also be sorted. Steps vary slightly from these.

In this example, the selected bulleted list will be sorted alphabetically from A to Z.

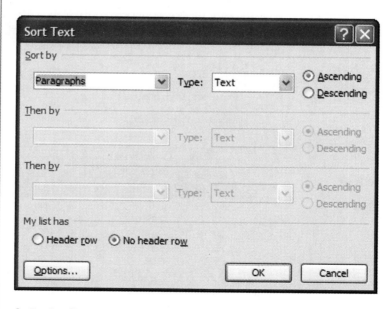

3. In the **Sort by** box, click **Paragraphs;** in the **Type** box, click **Text;** and click **Ascending.**

(continued on next page)

To undo a sort, click the **Undo** button immediately after sorting.

4. Click **OK.** The list is sorted alphabetically from A to Z.

- Bandwidth
- Bus width
- Data rate
- System clock

PRACTICE

1. Sort this list alphabetically in ascending order.

As you know, your health care plan will be changing effective April 1. In order to help you plan for any anticipated future expenses, you should go to your *Summary Plan Description* booklet and research the following topics:

- Dental plan program
- Pharmacy co-pay structure
- Member-managed care
- Deductibles
- Office visits

Please contact us if you have any questions at 800-555-1212.

2. Note the list after sorting. Your list should now look like this:

As you know, your health care plan will be changing effective April 1. In order to help you plan for any anticipated future expenses, you should go to your *Summary Plan Description* booklet and research the following topics:

- Deductibles
- Dental plan program
- Member-managed care
- Office visits
- Pharmacy co-pay structure

Please contact us if you have any questions at 800-555-1212.

 Textbook

3. Save changes to *practice-72*, and return to GDP.

More Special Letter Features

Shading

To give your table a more finished look, you can add shading.
   To add shading:

1. Select the desired cells.
2. From the **Home** tab, in the **Paragraph** group, click the list arrow to the right of the **Borders** button, and click **Borders and Shading** at the bottom of the list.

   Or: Right-click the selected cells and click **Borders and Shading**
   Note: The border that appears in the **Borders** button changes depending upon the last-used choice on the drop-down list.

3. From the **Borders** and **Shading** window, click the **Shading** tab.

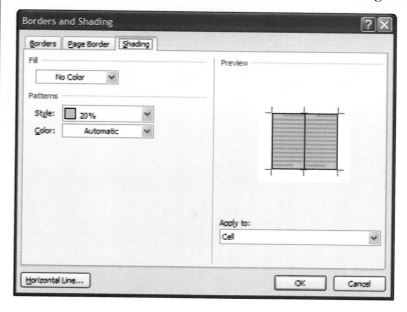

4. Select the shading option you want by clicking on the down arrow in the **Style** box. **Clear** (the default setting) provides no shading. **Solid** **(100%)** provides a solid black shading, with the text appearing in white. A **10%**, **20%**, or **25%** shading provides a light gray shading, with the black text still visible.
5. Click **OK**.

(continued on next page)

PRACTICE

1. Select Row 1 (containing the title and subtitle).
2. Right-click the selected row, and click **Borders and Shading.** From the **Borders and Shading** window, click the **Shading** tab, and apply a **Solid 100%** shading to Row 1 (black).
3. Apply 20% shading to Row 2 (column titles) and Row 7 (TOTAL). Your screen should now look like this:

Solid **(100%)** shading

(20%) shading

Clear shading

SERVICE DEPARTMENT PAYROLL Week Ending June 7, 20--			
Employee	Hours	Rate	Gross Pay
Luis J. Bachman	40.00	$ 8.93	$ 357.20
Austin Engerrand	18.25	7.80	142.35
Louise W. Vik	35.50	13.45	477.47
Robert Wendlinger	37.75	16.50	622.88
TOTAL			$1,599.90

4. Save the changes to *practice-73*, and return to GDP.

Go To Textbook

Multipage Memos With Tables

Find and Replace

You can use **Find** to search for text, numbers, etc., in a document. You can also use **Replace** to both find and replace the found text with revised text. For example, if you want to replace "James" with "Jim," you could replace all occurrences of the name in one step.

To find text:

1. From the **Home** tab, in the **Editing** group, click the **Find** button.

Or: On the keyboard, press CTRL + F.
The **Find and Replace** dialog box appears with the **Find** tab active.

Type the text you want to find in the **Find what** box.

Note: Click **More** to expand the dialog box and display other options.
Or: If the box is already expanded, click **Less** to collapse the box.

2. Type the text (or characters) you want to find in the **Find what** text box.
3. Click **Find Next.**
Note: If Word finds the text, it highlights that text in the document. You can edit the text without closing the **Find and Replace** dialog box and then continue the search by clicking **Find Next** again.
4. To close the dialog box, click **Cancel** or press ESC.

To find and replace text:

1. From the **Home** tab, in the **Editing** group, click the **Replace** button.

Or: From the keyboard, press CTRL + H.
The **Find and Replace** dialog box appears with the **Replace** tab active.

(continued on next page)

Type the text you want to find in the **Find what** text box and the replacement text in the **Replace with** text box.

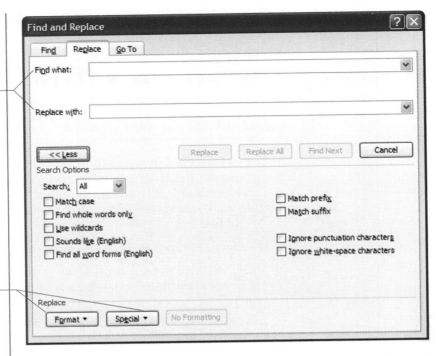

Click **Format** or **Special** to find and/or replace nonprinting characters (such as a tab character or a font change).

Note: Click **More** to expand the dialog box and display other options. **Or:** If the box is already expanded, click **Less** to collapse the box.

2. Type the text you want to replace in the **Find what** text box.
3. Press **Tab** and type the replacement text in the **Replace with** text box.
4. Click **Find Next.**
   Note: If Word finds the text, it highlights it in the document. To replace the text, click **Replace;** to leave it unchanged, click **Find Next.**
   Note: To automatically change all occurrences of the text in the document without stopping to verify each change, click **Replace All.**
5. When Word finishes, click **Cancel** or press **Esc.**

PRACTICE

1. Use **Replace** to find all occurrences of "United Manufacturing" and replace it with "Global Industrial."

   Note: You should have located and changed four occurrences.

2. Save changes to *practice-74*, and return to GDP.

Textbook

Tables With Footnotes or Source Notes

Table—Text Direction

Text Direction button

Text Direction button set to vertical from bottom to top

The default orientation for text in a table is horizontal. Sometimes, however, you may want to align text in a table vertically such as for long column headings.

To change the text direction or orientation of text in a table:

1. Click the cell or select the row that contains the text to be changed.
2. Under **Table Tools**, on the **Layout** tab, in the **Alignment** group, click the **Text Direction** button repeatedly until you see the desired text direction. Notice that the **Text Direction** button changes to give you a preview of the alignment.
3. Click the **Align Bottom Left** button.
4. Point to the bottom border of the row containing the vertical text until you see the resize pointer; drag down until the text appears in one continuous line without wrapping.

PRACTICE

1. Select Row 1.
2. Change the text direction to position the column headings vertically from bottom to top. Your table should appear similar to the one below:

Sailing Departures	Interior Stateroom	Ocean View Stateroom	Additional Guest
5/24	$699	$799	$299
6/31	799	899	350
7/7	899	999	400

3. Drag down on the bottom border of Row 1 until the column headings appear in one continuous line without wrapping.
4. Click inside the table and apply the **AutoFit to Contents** feature.

(continued on next page)

5. Center the table horizontally and vertically. Your table should appear similar to the one below:

Sailing Departures	Interior Stateroom	Ocean View Stateroom	Additional Guest
5/24	$699	$799	$299
6/31	799	899	350
7/7	899	999	400

Table Resize Handle

6. Save all changes to *practice-76*.

Note: Keep this document open, and continue reading below.

Table—Insert or Delete Rows or Columns

Before you can insert or delete rows or columns, you must first select the row or column. Word inserts a new row or column either above, below, left, or right as you choose.

> **Note:** Under **Table Tools,** on the **Layout** tab, you will see **Insert Above**, **Insert Below**, **Insert Left**, and **Insert Right** buttons to insert rows and columns.

To insert a row:

1. Select the desired row.

Sailing Departures	Interior Stateroom	Ocean View Stateroom	Additional Guest
5/24	$699	$799	$299
6/31	799	899	350
7/7	899	999	400

Move the mouse over the selection bar area to the left of the row you want to select until you see the diagonal arrow, then click the row to select it.

(continued on next page)

2. With the row still selected, click the right mouse button to open the shortcut menu; then click **Insert**, **Insert Rows Above** (or the appropriate choice.)

Click **Insert, Insert Rows Above** from the shortcut menu.

A new blank row appears *above* the selected row.

To insert a column:

1. Select the desired column.

Point to the top border of the column you want to select and click to select the column.

To insert a new row at the end of a table, click in the last cell (cell D4 in this case) and press **TAB**.

(continued on next page)

2. With the column still selected, click the right mouse button to open the shortcut menu; then click **Insert**, **Insert Columns to the Left** (or the appropriate choice).

Sailing Departures	Interior Stateroom	Ocean View Stateroom	Additional Guest
5/24	$699	$799	$299
6/29	759	859	325
7/7	899	999	400

To delete a row or column:

1. Select the desired row or column.
2. Click the right mouse button to open the shortcut menu.
3. Click **Delete Rows** or **Delete Columns** or press **Ctrl+X.**

PRACTICE *(continued)*

1. Insert a new row above Row 3
2. Type the following information in the new row.

   6/29   759   859   325

3. Delete Row 4 with the sailing departure date of 6/31, and insert a new column to the left of Column D.
4. Type the following information in the new column. Type 3 spaces after the dollar sign.

   Junior Suite $899   959   1,099

5. Insert a new row at the end of the table.
6. Merge the cells in the new row.
7. Type Note: Prices may vary., and change the alignment to left. Your table should appear similar to the one below:

Sailing Departures	Interior Stateroom	Ocean View Stateroom	Junior Suite	Additional Guest
5/24	$699	$799	$ 899	$299
6/29	759	859	959	325
7/7	899	999	1,099	400
Note: Prices may vary.				

8. Save all changes to *practice-76*, and return to GDP.

Tables Formatted Sideways

Page Orientation

The default page orientation for 8.5- × 11-inch paper is vertical (also known as *portrait*). Sometimes, however, the content of a document would fit better or appear more attractive in horizontal orientation (called *landscape*).

Portrait orientation

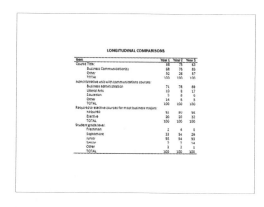

Landscape orientation

To change the page orientation:

1. On the **Page Layout** tab, in the **Page Setup** group, click the **Orientation** button, and click either **Portrait** or **Landscape**.

Or: In **Print Preview** in the **Page Setup** group, click the **Orientation** button, and click either **Portrait** or **Landscape**.

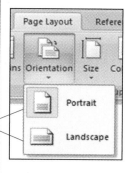

Click either **Portrait** (vertical) or **Landscape** (horizontal) orientation.

(continued on next page)

PRACTICE

1. Change the page orientation to **Landscape**.

2. Switch to **Print Preview**. Your document should look like this:

LONGITUDINAL COMPARISONS

Item	Year 1	Year 2	Year 3
Course Title:	68	75	63
Business Communication(s)	68	75	63
Other	32	26	37
TOTAL	100	100	100
Administrative unit with communications courses:			
Business administration	71	78	69
Liberal Arts	10	8	17
Education	5	8	8
Other	14	6	5
TOTAL	100	100	100
Required or elective courses for most business majors:			
Required	81	80	68
Elective	20	20	32
TOTAL	100	100	100
Student grade level:			
Freshman	2	4	3
Sophomore	33	34	29
Junior	55	54	53
Senior	7	7	14
Other	2	2	1
TOTAL	100	100	100

Go To Textbook

3. Save the changes to *practice-78*, and return to GDP.

Multipage Tables

Table—Repeating Table Heading Rows

The second page of most multipage tables will not make sense to the reader unless the table heading rows are repeated on each page. Consider, for example, the following 2-page table:

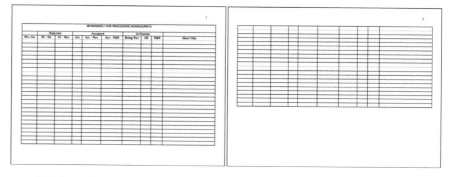

Without headings, page 2 is just a series of empty cells.
To repeat a table heading on subsequent pages:

1. Select the rows of text (including the first row) that you want to use as a table heading.

WORKSHEET FOR PROCESSING MANUSCRIPTS									
	Rejected		Accepted			In Process			
Ms. No.	RJ—Ed	RJ—Rev	Acc	Acc—Rev	Acc—R&R	Being Rev	AR	R&R	Short Title

2. Under **Table Tools**, on the **Layout** tab, in the **Data** group, click **Repeat Header Rows**.
The headings are now repeated on each page.

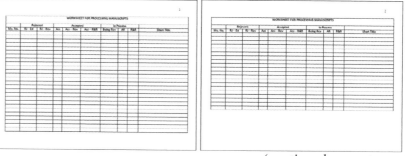

(continued on next page)

PRACTICE

1. Select the first three rows of the table; under **Table Tools,** on the **Layout** tab, in the **Data** group, click **Repeat Header Rows.**
2. Scroll down to page 2 of the table. It should look similar to the following illustration.

2

WORKSHEET FOR PROCESSING MANUSCRIPTS									
	Rejected		Accepted			In Process			
Ms. No.	RJ—Ed	RJ—Rev	Acc	Acc—Rev	Acc—R&R	Being Rev	AR	R&R	Short Title

Go To Textbook

3. Save changes to *practice-79*, and return to GDP.

Using Predesigned Table Formats

Table—Styles

The **Table Styles** feature is used to quickly format a table with headings, borders, shading, etc. You can choose from a wide variety of styles, and choose the one that is most attractive in your document.

To format a table automatically:

1. Click anywhere in the table, and change your **Zoom** level so that your table is positioned at the bottom of the window. This will make it easier to see the **Live Preview.**

2. From the **Table Tools,** click the **Design** tab. From the **Table Styles** group, click the **More** list arrow.

3. Point to each style, look at the **Live Preview** in the table, and click the desired style.

More list arrow

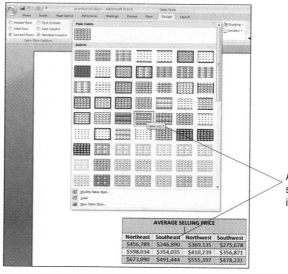

As you point to each **Built-In** style, note the **Live Preview** in your table below.

4. Under **Table Tools,** on the **Layout** tab, in the **Table Style Options** group, check and uncheck **Header Row, Total Row, Banded Rows, First Column, Last Column,** and **Banded Columns**; watch the **Live Preview** and check or uncheck the boxes as desired.

Note: As you point to each button, a descriptive screen tip will appear to help you make an educated choice.

(continued on next page)

Note: To clear a table style, do this: From the **Table Tools**, click the **Design** tab. From the **Table Styles** group, click the **More** list arrow. Click **Clear** at the bottom of the style list.

☐ Header Row	☐ First Column
☐ Total Row	☐ Last Column
☑ Banded Rows	☑ Banded Columns
Table Style Options	

Note: You might need to center the table horizontally and change cell alignment and font size after applying a table style.

PRACTICE

1. Apply the Table List 7 style (or any desired style) to this table. You will see the style name appear when you point to a style and pause briefly until the screen tip appears. Your table should appear similar to the one below:

AVERAGE SELLING PRICE

Northeast	Southeast	Northwest	Southwest
$456,789	$246,890	$369,135	$275,678
$598,034	$354,035	$410,239	$356,871
$673,090	$491,444	$555,397	$478,231

2. Center the table horizontally.
3. Right-align all column headings and column entries and change fonts and font sizes as needed.
4. Save all changes to *practice-80*, and return to GDP.

Textbook

Formal Report Project

Styles

A *style* is a set of formatting commands (fonts, indents, etc.) with an assigned name such as Heading 1 or Title. You can easily apply any style with all its formatting to the text in one step. Later, if you modify the style, all of the text to which that style has been assigned will automatically reflect the changes.

Every paragraph in a Word document has a paragraph style applied to it. The default style is called the *Normal* style.

The **Normal** style is the default style shown in the **Styles** group above. The order of the style buttons may vary. Click the **More** arrow to see a complete list.

To apply a style:

1. Position the insertion point in the paragraph where you want the style formatting to take effect, or select the text to which you want to apply a style.
2. From the **Home** tab, click the **Styles Dialog Box Launcher.**
3. From the bottom of the **Styles** pane, click **Options**.
4. From the **Style Pane Options** window, in the **Select styles to show** box, click the list arrow, **All Styles, OK**.
5. Click the desired style from the **Styles** pane and then click the **Close** button on the **Styles** pane to close it.

(continued on next page)

Or:

1. From the **Home** tab, in the **Styles** group, click the desired style; click the **More** button to see additional styles in the **Quick Styles** gallery.
2. Point to each style to see a **Live Preview** in your selected text or paragraph; then click the desired style.

Point to the desired style in the **Quick Style** gallery, and note the **Live Preview** in your document.

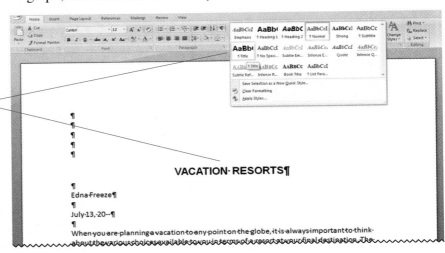

Selected (highlighted) text will take on the formatting characteristics of the applied style, or any new text you type will be formatted according to the style.

Note: If you are applying a style to new text, when you press **ENTER** you will return to the **Normal** style.

Note: To remove a style, select the affected text. From the **Home** tab, click the **Styles Diagonal Box Launcher**. From the **Styles** box, click **Normal**. Click the **Close** button on the **Styles** box.

PRACTICE

1. Apply the **Title** style to the report title.
2. Apply the **Subtitle** style to the report subtitle and date. (*Hint*: Click **More** to see additional styles.
3. Apply the **Heading 2** style to the three side headings.

   Note: Before you begin the steps below, do this: From the **Page Layout** tab, click the **Page Setup Dialog Box Launcher**, and then click the **Layout** tab. Under **Headers and footers**, verify that **Different first page** is *unchecked;* click **OK.**

4. Create a header to display on the second page only. Click anywhere on the first page of the document.
5. From the **Insert** tab, **Header & Footer** group, click the **Header** button; click **Blank**.

(continued on next page)

6. You will see [Type text] highlighted. Type `Vacation Resorts`, and press **TAB** twice to move to the right margin. Type `Page` and press the **SPACE BAR** once.

7. From the **Design** tab, **Header & Footer** group, click **Page Number**, **Current Position**, **Plain Number**. (*Hint*: If the wrong page number is displayed, do this: from the **Insert** tab, in the **Header & Footer** group, click **Page Number**. Click **Format Page Numbers**. In the **Start at** box, type the desired number; click **OK**.)

8. Press **CTRL + A** to select all text; then press **CTRL + I** to italicize all header text and change the font to 10-point Cambria.

9. Press the right arrow on the keyboard to deselect the text and to move to the line below the header.

10. To add a bottom border, from the **Home** tab, **Paragraph** group, click the list arrow on the **Borders** button, and click the **Bottom Border** button.

11. From the **Design** tab, click **Different First Page**.

   Note: You should now be in the **First Page Header** section and it should be blank. If the page number is still in the **First Page Header**, select the page number and cut it.

12. Scroll down to the second page to see the header, which should now have text, a page number, and a bottom border.

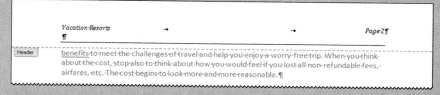

13. Double-click inside the document to close the header. Your report should appear similar to the one below.

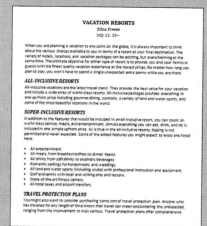

14. Save all changes to *practice-81*, and return to GDP.

Formal Report Project

Insert Clip Art and Files

One of the easiest ways to make a document interesting is to add a graphic or picture. Pictures can be sized easily and positioned within a document.

Many different graphics (clip art images) are available to you in Word. You may also use other available clip art images as long as they are compatible with Word.

To add a picture to a document:

Clip Art button

1. Click in the document where you want to insert clip art.
2. From the **Insert** tab, in the **Illustrations** group, click the **Clip Art** button.
3. Note that a **Clip Art** task pane opens on the right of the Word window.

Clip Art task pane

4. In the **Clip Art** task pane, in the **Search for** box, type a word or phrase describing the type of clip you want.

Note: Click the down arrow in the **Search in** text box to specify the collections to search. You can also specify the type of media file in the **Results should be** text box.

(continued on next page)

5. Click **Go.**

Clip Art task pane after
searching for "resort."

6. Scroll down to view the displayed clip art.

7. Click the picture you want to insert, and it will be inserted automatically.

To find more clip art:

Clip art on Office Online button

1. Click the **Clip art on Office Online** button at the bottom of the **Clip Art** task pane.

Note: You must have an Internet connection at this point.

2. Follow the steps there to search for additional clip art.

To position the picture:

1. Click the picture to select it. The **Picture Tools Format** tab appears on demand.

Text Wrapping button

2. From the **Arrange** group, click the **Text Wrapping** button; click **Square** or right-click the selected picture, and click **Text Wrapping, Square.** This text wrapping will wrap text all around the picture on all sides depending where you position it.

Note: If you need to drag the picture freely and wrapping text around the clip art does not apply in the current document, right-click the selected picture, and click **Text Wrapping, In Front of Text.** You can now drag the picture and drop it into position anywhere on the page.
Note: By default, picture text wrapping is set to **In Line With Text.** This text wrapping style makes a picture move just like an additional keystroke in a line. To change an inline picture to a floating picture that can be dragged freely, you must select a wrapping style.

4-headed pointer for moving

3. Position the mouse pointer over the selected graphic until it changes to a 4-headed pointer.

(continued on next page)

4. Drag the graphic to position.

Note: If you drag clip art in place, but it doesn't seem to anchor securely to that spot, do this: With the picture selected, right-click and click **Text Wrapping.** From the expanded shortcut menu, click **More Layout Options**. From the **Advanced Layout** window, in the **Picture Position** tab under **Options**, check **Move object with text**, and click **OK**. You can now move your image wherever you want on the page and it should stay anchored in place.

To size the picture:

1. Select the picture by clicking it.
2. Position the mouse pointer over a sizing handle until the pointer turns into a 2-headed arrow.

Note: Use one of the 4-corner sizing handles to prevent the picture from being distorted when it is resized.

2-headed pointer for sizing

3. Drag the sizing handle and notice that a shadow of the picture appears. The box represents the new size. Release the mouse button.

A selected picture has sizing handles.

Drag one of the top or bottom sizing handles to adjust the height.

Drag one of the middle sizing handles to adjust the width.

Drag one of the corner sizing handles to adjust the width and height and to maintain the original proportions.

Note: A second way to size a picture is to right-click it, click **Size**; from the **Size** tab under **Size and Rotate**, type the desired size in either the **Height** or **Width** box, and click **Close**. The picture will be resized proportionately to the measurement entered in either the **Height** or **Width** box.

Under the **Format** tab, experiment freely with all the buttons and tools in these groups: **Adjust, Picture Styles, Arrange**, and **Size**. In the **Picture Styles** group, the **Picture Effects** buttons can give you some of the most dramatic effects of all. In the **Adjust** group, try the **Recolor** button. In the **Arrange Group**, the **Rotate** button allows you to turn your picture. You also can rotate using the green rotate dot at the top of a picture. In the **Size** group, the crop tool allows you to "cut" part of your picture. You'll be surprised at the many interesting effects you can create.

(continued on next page)

Right-click a selected picture to edit it. Experiment freely with these **Format Picture** options. Click **Reset Picture** to undo any changes.

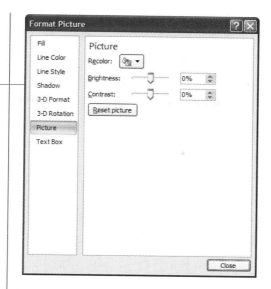

PRACTICE

1. Click in front of the first word in the first paragraph.
2. Insert a picture related to resorts.
3. Change the wrap style to **Square.**
4. Set the picture width to approximately 1 inch.
5. Drag the picture so that it is positioned at the right margin of the first paragraph.

Your document should look similar to this:

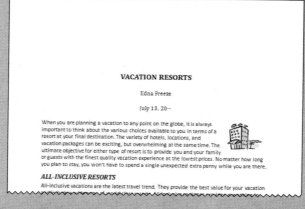

6. Save changes to *practice-83*.

Note: Keep this document open, and continue reading below.

(continued on next page)

INSERT A FILE

There may be times when you want to insert the contents of one Word document into another. To insert a Word document into the current active document:

1. Position the insertion point where you want the contents of the inserted file to appear.

2. From the **Insert** tab, in the **Text** group, click the arrow next to the **Object** button, and then click **Text from File**.

Note: Be sure to click the arrow next to the **Object** button and *not* the **Object** button itself.

The **Insert File** dialog box appears.

Click here to browse to a different drive.

If the folder or file you want to open is displayed, double-click to open it.

3. Click the list arrow next to the **Look in** box to browse to the desired location.

4. Double-click the desired file name to insert the document at the insertion point.

Note: In the **Files of types** box, click the list arrow and click **All Files** (*.*) to display all files if necessary. This step is very important when inserting any file with an extension other than docx.

PRACTICE *(continued)*

1. Position the insertion point at the end of the report, and press **ENTER** 2 times.

2. Insert the file named *practice-83-Insert.docx*. You will see it in the file list. The second page of your document should look similar to this:

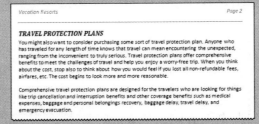

3. Save the changes to *practice-83*, and return to GDP.

Textbook

International Formatting (Canada)

Paper Size

The default paper size is the standard 8.5 × 11 inches. You can, however, change the paper size if your printer has the capability of handling different-sized paper.

To change the paper size:

1. From the **Page Layout** tab, in the **Page Setup** group, click the **Size** button.
2. From the expanded list, click the desired paper size.
3. If the size you want is not listed, click **More Paper Sizes** at the bottom of the list.

A4 metric paper size has been selected.

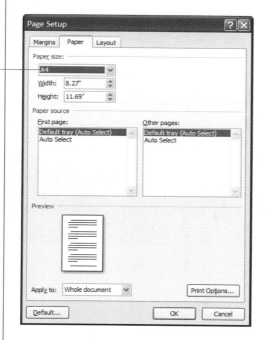

4. To select a custom size of paper (for example, half-page size, or 5.5 × 8.5 inches), click the list arrow under **Paper size**, and then scroll down and click **Custom size**. Change the **Width** and **Height** to the appropriate sizes.

(continued on next page)

Type in the desired paper
dimension.

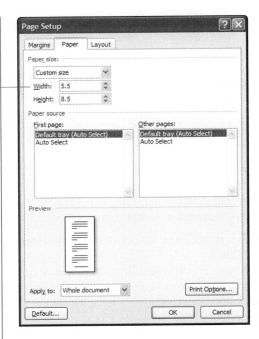

5. Click **OK**.

PRACTICE

1. Change the paper size to **A4**.

2. Add an envelope to the document using the **DL** envelope size option.

(**Hint**: From the **Mailings** tab, click **Envelopes**; click **Options** on the **Envelopes** tab; click the **Envelope Options** tab, and click the down arrow next to the **Envelope size** box; scroll down the list, click **DL**, and click **OK**; click **Add to Document**.)

Go To Textbook

3. Save the changes to *practice-86*, and return to GDP.

International Formatting (Mexico)

Insert Symbol

Many foreign languages use diacritical marks or a combination of characters to indicate phonetic sounds. The **Symbol** dialog box contains many of the characters needed to type words with special accents.

To insert a symbol:

1. Click where you want to insert a symbol, or select an existing letter.
2. From the **Insert** tab, **Symbols** group, click the **Symbol** button, **More Symbols**.

An international character can be inserted by using a shortcut key. Microsoft Word Help provides a list of symbols and shortcut keys.

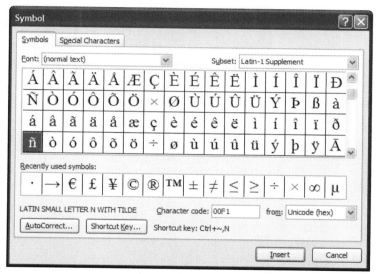

3. In the **Font** box, click (normal text).
4. In the **Subset** box, click **Latin-1 Supplement** to move to a character code subset for the desired symbol.
5. Scroll down if needed until you see the desired symbol.
6. Click a symbol to see a highlighted view.
7. Click **Insert** to insert the symbol and click **Close**.

   Note: After you click **Insert**, your symbol is automatically added to the **Recently used symbols** area under the **Symbols** button for easy insertion next time.

8. Check the capitalization of the symbol. It may be necessary to change from uppercase to lowercase.

(continued on next page)

PRACTICE

1. Your practice file will open as shown below without any special symbols.

Symbol	Spanish Word	English Translation
n	Senor	Mr.
	Senorita	Mrs.
i	el rio	River
o	adios	goodbye

2. Insert symbols as shown in the table below until your table looks like this one.

Symbol	Spanish Word	English Translation
ñ	Señor	Mr.
	Señorita	Mrs.
í	el río	River
ó	adiós	goodbye

3. Save the changes to *practice-87*, and return to GDP.

Textbook

Legal Office Applications

Line Numbering

To number lines in a document—for example, in legal documents for reference in a court of law—you can use Word's line numbering command. Line numbers can be positioned, formatted, and turned on or off as needed. Line numbers can also be restarted within a document.

Word can add line numbers to every line in the document and restart line numbering on each page.

To begin line numbering:

1. Position the insertion point at the start of the page where you want line numbering to begin.
2. Click the **Zoom** level button from the bottom of the window, and change the zoom setting to **Page width** so that you will be able to see the line numbering in the space between the left edge of the page and the left margin.

Zoom level button

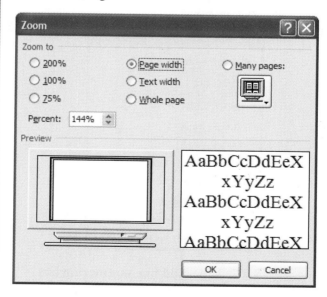

(continued on next page)

3. From the **Page Layout** tab, **Page Setup** group, click the **Line Numbers** button. Click **Line Numbering Options** at the bottom of the expanded list.

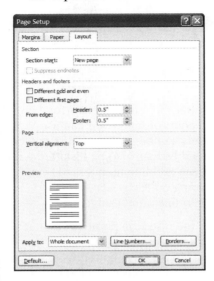

4. Click the **Layout** tab, and click the **Line Numbers** button. The **Line Numbers** dialog box appears.

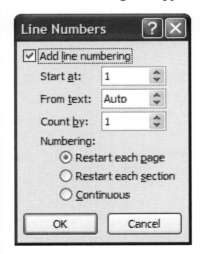

5. Click the **Add line numbering** box.

Note: The rest of the default settings are already correct for standard line numbering.

6. Click **OK** twice.

(continued on next page)

PRACTICE

1. If necessary, change to **Print Layout** view, and change the zoom to **Page width**.
2. Add line numbering. Your document should look like this:

```
 1                        AFFIDAVIT OF POSSESSION
 2
 3    STATE OF CALIFORNIA
 4
 5    COUNTY OF LOS ANGELES
 6
 7            Steve Broers, being first duly sworn, deposes and says:
 8
 9            That he is an adult person and is a resident of Los Angeles County, California, and
10    that his mailing address is P.O. Box 1219, Valencia, CA 91355.
11
12            That he knows the history, ownership, and occupancy of the following-described
13    property situated in Los Angeles County, California, to-wit:
14
15            All that part of the Southeast Quarter of the Northeast Quarter of Section Nine
16            (9), Township Seventy-two (72), further described as follows: Beginning at the Northeast
17            corner of said Southeast Quarter of the Northeast Quarter; thence South along the East
18            line of said quarter 1000.00 feet; thence west 575.00 feet; thence North 200.00 feet;
19            thence West 204.00 feet; thence North 800.00 feet; thence East 979.00 feet.
20
21            That the record title holder in fee simple of the above property is Steve Broers, a
22            single person; that he is presently in possession of the above-described premises;
23
24            That ownership of the aforesaid property is based upon an unbroken chain of
25            title through immediate and remote grantors by deed of conveyance which has been
26            recorded since December 19, 1984, at 2 a.m.;
27
28            That the purpose of this Affidavit of Possession is to show proof of ownership by
29    providing and recording evidence of possession for marketable title as required by the
30    Marketable Record Title Act of the State of California.
31
32            DATED this _____ day of August, 2006, at Valencia, California.
33
34
35                                          Shannon Dear                Attorney-at-Law
36
37    Subscribed and sworn to before me this _____ day of August, 2006.
38
39
40                                          Denise Clooney              Notary Public
41                                          Los Angeles County, California
42                                          My Commission Expires July 17, 2012
```

Go To — Textbook

3. Save changes to *practice-96*, and return to GDP.

Using Correspondence Templates

Correspondence Templates

Every document that you create is based on a normal template that defines margins, tab settings, toolbars displayed, and additional formatting. When you start Word and begin typing in the document window, you are using Word's default template, called the *normal* template.

Instead of using the normal template, you can create a document by opening any one of Word's predefined document templates. You might want to use one of Word's correspondence templates such as a memo or letter template.

Note: Because Microsoft adds and removes templates frequently and their availability is unpredictable, you will not select a template in the usual way. Instead, when you complete your document processing jobs and these practice exercises, GDP will automatically open a preselected blank document template ready for input. However, the steps to open a template in Word under normal conditions are presented in this lesson.

To use a memo template:

1. Click the **Microsoft Office Button**; then click the **New** button.
2. In the **New Document** window, under **Microsoft Office Online**, click **Memos** (or click the desired template category).

   Note: Under **Templates**, browse **Installed Templates** and **My templates** for other choices.

3. Under the **Memos** pane (or the desired category), click the desired template, and note the preview in the right pane.

   Note: To use a letter template, click the **Microsoft Office Button**, and click the **New** button. In the **New Document** window, from the **Search Microsoft Office for a template** box, type letterhead and press **ENTER**. Under **Search results**, click the desired **Letterhead** design template.

(continued on next page)

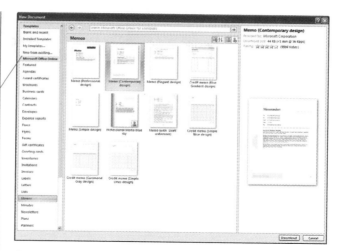

Click any desired template category under **Microsoft Office Online** to search online for a template.

4. Click **Download**. The predefined document appears.

> **Note:** If you see a **Microsoft Genuine Advantage** window, click **Continue** to validate the status of your Microsoft Office software.

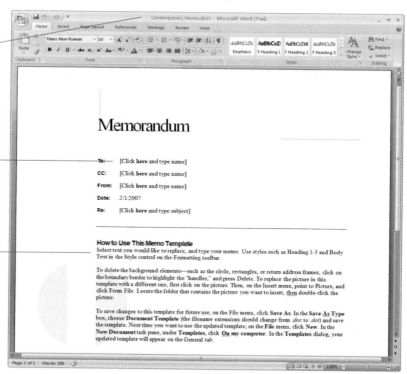

Word assigns a temporary file name until you save your document.

Click to select the temporary placeholder text in brackets, and replace it with your own text. Delete any unwanted text.

Read and follow any directions included with the template. The body style of many templates often inserts extra space between paragraphs. You generally press **ENTER** only once between paragraphs.

5. Click the text in brackets to select it, then type your replacement text.

6. Select and delete any parts of the template text you don't want to use; for example, you might want to delete the *Confidential* text box at the bottom of the page.

(continued on next page)

7. Read the instructions on the template and follow any that apply.
8. Save the document as you normally would. After you finish using this template, the top part of the completed memo should look similar to this:

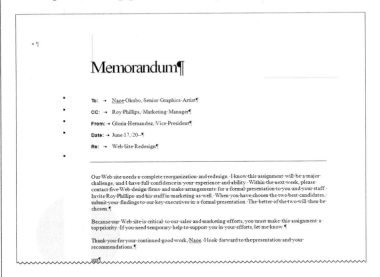

PRACTICE

1. Note that a memo template has opened automatically, ready for your input, and has already been assigned a name.
2. Type a memo to Helen Lalin with a copy to Jose Limon from you. The date is February 14, 20— and the subject line (Re:) is Luncheon Invitation.

   Note: When you click the placeholder text *[Click here and type name]*, the placeholder will be selected. As you begin typing, the placeholder will be replaced with your text. When you click the field next to the date heading, you will see a date update field. Drag across the field from the start to the end, delete it, and type in the desired date.
   Note: When you use a letter template in GDP, and are ready to type the salutation, turn on **Show/Hide**. Click the salutation field, drag across the field from the start to the end excluding the paragraph mark, delete it, and type in the salutation. When you click the complimentary closing field, drag across the field from the start to the end excluding the paragraph mark, delete the selected text, and type in the complimentary closing.

3. Move to the bottom of the page, click the text box frame with the *Confidential* notation to select it, and press **DELETE**. Open the footer pane, click the frame on the shaded rectangle to select it, and press **DELETE**.

(continued on next page)

4. Select the body of the memo from the first bold line of the memo template instructions to the end of the last paragraph of instructions. Begin typing the first paragraph of the memo body just after selecting the memo instructions *without* pressing **DELETE.** (If you delete the selected instructions, you could delete the embedded paragraph styles.)

```
I will be happy to attend the luncheon meeting
of the Purchasing Managers' Association with you
next Tuesday at the Friar's Club. Since I'll be
at a workshop until 11:15 that morning, I'll
meet you in the lobby of the Friar's Club at
12:15 p.m.

Thanks for thinking of me.
```

Note: When you press **ENTER** at the end of the first paragraph, an extra blank line should be inserted automatically. If it is not added, press **ENTER** as needed to insert 1 blank line between paragraphs.

5. Press **ENTER** 1 time after typing the body and type your reference initials. Your document should look similar to this:

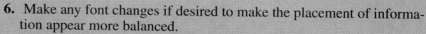

Memorandum

To: Helen Lalic
CC: Jose Limon
From: Student Name
Date: February 14, 20--
Re: Luncheon Invitation

I will be happy to attend the luncheon meeting of the Purchasing Managers' Association with you next Tuesday at the Friar's Club. Since I'll be at a workshop until 11:15 that morning, I'll meet you in the lobby of the Friar's Club at 12:15 p.m.

Thanks for thinking of me

urs

6. Make any font changes if desired to make the placement of information appear more balanced.

7. Save the file as *practice-101*, and return to GDP.

Go To Textbook

Using Report Templates

Report Templates

Note: Because Microsoft adds and removes templates frequently and their availability is unpredictable, you will not select a template in the usual way. Instead, when you complete your document processing jobs and these practice exercises, GDP will automatically open a preselected blank document template ready for input. However, the steps to open a template in Word under normal conditions are presented in this lesson.

To use a report template:

1. Click the **Microsoft Office Button**; then click the **New** button.
2. In the **New Document** window, under **Microsoft Office Online**, click **Reports** (or click the desired template category).

   Note: Under **Templates**, browse **Installed Templates** and **My templates** for other choices.

3. Under the **Reports** pane (or the desired category), click the desired template, and note the preview in the right pane.

Click any desired report in the **Reports** pane.

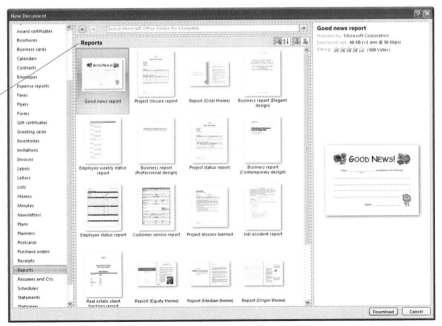

(continued on next page)

4. Click **Download**. The predefined document appears

    Note: If you see a **Microsoft Genuine Advantage** window, click **Continue** to validate the status of your Microsoft Office software.

5. Click the text in brackets to select it, and type your replacement text.
6. Select and delete any parts of the template text you don't want to use.
7. Read the instructions on the template and follow any that apply.
8. Save the document as you normally would.

PRACTICE

1. Note that a report template has opened automatically, ready for your input, and has already been assigned a name. The first page looks like this:

> Type Address Here
>
> blue sky associates
>
> **FilmWatch Division**
> **Marketing Plan**
>
> *Trey's Best Opportunity to Dominate*
> *Market Research for the Film Industry*

2. Click the *Type Address Here* placeholder to select it, and type the following:

```
4066 Main Avenue
Orlando, Florida 32806
```

    Note: As you begin typing, the placeholder will be replaced with your text.

(continued on next page)

3. Select the company name *blue sky associates*, and type `Digital Media`.
4. Select the title *FilmWatch Division Marketing Plan*, and type `New Technologies`.
5. Select the subtitle *Trey's Best Opportunity to Dominate Market Research for the Film Industry*, and press the **SPACE BAR** once to delete it.
6. Move to the second page of the report, replace the title with the same one used on the first page, and delete the subtitle.
7. Select the first side heading *How To Use This Report Template*, and type `Introduction`.
8. Select the first paragraph only under the Introduction section, and type this:

   `Digital Media will soon introduce an exciting new line of products.`

9. Select from the beginning of the second paragraph to the end of the second bulleted item just before the second side heading, and delete it.

   Note: The remaining pages in the report template would be completed in a similar manner. If you need to add additional side headings and text, select existing ones; then copy, paste, and edit them. If a **Paste Options** box appears, click **Keep Text Only** so that pasted text will take on the template's styles.

   The first two pages of your unfinished report should look similar to the following:

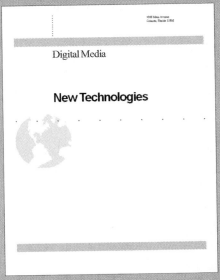

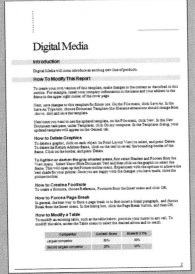

Textbook

10. Save the unfinished report as *practice-102*, and return to GDP.

Designing Letterheads

Small Caps

You can vary the appearance of text by changing the font to small caps. The first column below illustrates words typed in all caps, initial caps, and lowercase. The second column illustrates the same text with the small caps effect applied to it.

Normal	Small Caps
ALL CAPS	ALL CAPS
Initial Caps	INITIAL CAPS
lowercase	LOWERCASE

To apply small caps:

1. Position the insertion point where you want to begin using small caps (or select the text you want to change).
2. From the **Home** tab, click the **Font Dialog Box Launcher**.
3. When the **Font** dialog box appears, check **Small caps**; then click **OK**.

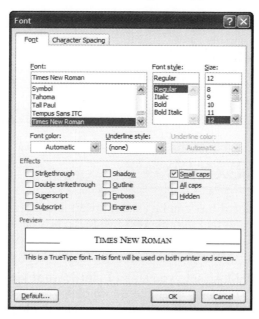

(continued on next page)

PRACTICE

1. With **Show/Hide** on and the ruler displayed (click the **View Ruler** button), press **ENTER** 6 times.
2. Type `Employee`, press **ENTER**, and type `Benefit Plan` on the next line.
3. Select both lines, center them, and apply the small caps font with a 36-pt. font size. Your document should look similar to this:

Click the **View Ruler** button to display the ruler and click it again to hide the ruler.

4. Save changes to *practice-103,* and continue reading below.

Text Boxes

Print Layout view button   **Zoom** level button

A text box can be used to insert and emphasize text (for example, an important quote). Text inside the box can be formatted, the borders and fill can be changed, and the box can be positioned and sized freely.

To add a text box to a document:

1. Make sure you are in **Print Layout** view; then click the **Zoom** level button to open the **Zoom** dialog box.
2. In the **Zoom** dialog box, click **Whole page** and note the preview; click **OK**.

(continued on next page)

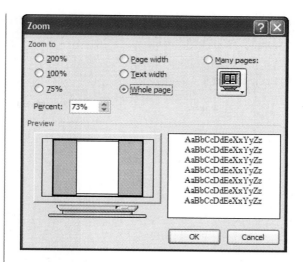

3. From the **Insert** tab, **Text** group, click the **Text Box** button; then click the **Draw Text Box** button at the bottom of the list.

Note: If you are inside a table cell and insert a text box with the **Built-In** text box choices, the text box can sometimes be locked inside the cell. To avoid this, click above the table or just under the last row of the table. Then you can drag your text box freely over the table or anywhere on the page.

Text Box button

Draw Text Box button

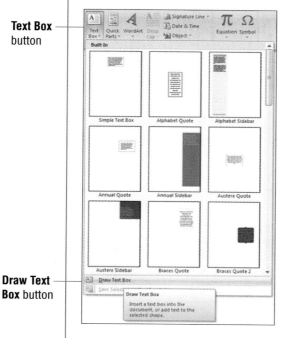

(continued on next page)

4. To create the text box, position the cross hair where you want the text box to appear; then drag to create the text box.

Use the white section of the displayed rulers to help you draw your box to the approximate desired size. This box is about 4 inches wide and 2 inches high.

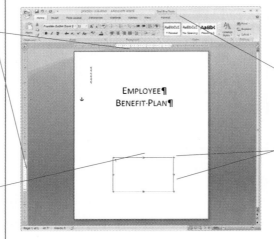

A **Text Box Tools** tab with a **Format** tab below it appears on demand when you draw a text box.

sizing handles.

An outline of the text box appears with blue sizing handles when the text box is selected.

+

Cross hair pointer

Note: An on-demand **Text Box Tools** tab appears with related commands below it in the **Format** tab after you draw or select a text box.

5. Change the **Zoom** level to **Page width**.

6. Click within the text box to make it active. (Blue dotted borders and sizing handles appear in an active text box when you're inside the box ready for editing.)

7. Type and format the desired text inside the box, and click outside the box when you're finished.

Note: If the text does not fit within the box, you must manually resize the box.

To position and size the text box:

1. Change the **Zoom** level to **Page width**. Then click the text box border to select the text box. Notice the difference between the appearance of the text box border when you select the border versus the appearance of the text box border when you click within a text box for text editing.

Sun Industries
759 Wilshire Boulevard
Los Angeles, CA 90017

Text box with border selected

Sun Industries
759 Wilshire Boulevard
Los Angeles, CA 90017

Text box ready for text editing with insertion point inside

(continued on next page)

Positioning pointer

If you lose sight of the desired text box, change the **Zoom** level to **Page width** or click the **Zoom Out** (minus button) or **Zoom In** (plus button) button or drag the **Zoom** slider.

2. Position the mouse pointer on one of the outer edges of the text box until the pointer changes to a 4-headed positioning pointer.

Note: Blue sizing handles will appear on the edges of the text box when it has been selected.

Drag one of the top or bottom sizing handles to adjust the height.

Drag one of the middle sizing handles to adjust the width.

Drag one of the corner sizing handles to adjust the width and height in one step.

Resize pointer

3. Position the mouse pointer on a sizing handle until the pointer changes to a 2-headed resize pointer; then drag to size the box. Repeat this step for all sides of the box.

4. Drag the text box to position it. (An outline of the box will appear as you drag it.)

Note: Once a text box is selected, you can also use the directional arrows or **CTRL+** directional arrows to position the box. Or under the **Text Box Tools** tab, click the **Format** tab; under the **Arrange** group, click the **Align** button and click the desired alignment. To anchor the text box so it moves with a certain line on a page, select the text box and click **Show/Hide**. Look in the left margin area until you see the black anchor. Drag the anchor and drop it next to the desired line and your text box will move with this line.

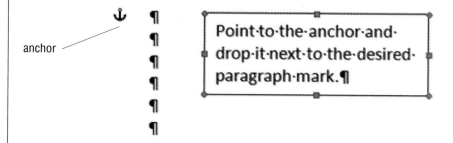

(continued on next page)

To change the outline of a text box:

1. Select the text box.
2. Under the **Text Box Tools** tab, click the **Format** tab.
3. Under the **Text Box Styles** group, click the **Shape Outline** button and click the desired color, width, and line style. If you want to remove the border, click **No Outline**.

Note: Remember to use the **Live Preview** feature as you point to each choice so that you can see the effect of each choice on your text box before you click your final selection.

Text Box Tools Format tab

To change the fill in a text box:

1. Select the text box.
2. Under the **Text Box Tools** tab, click the **Format** tab.
3. Under the **Text Box Styles** group, click the **Shape Fill** button and click the desired solid color, gradient, picture, or texture.

To change the overall visual text box style:

1. Select the text box.
2. Under the **Text Box Tools** tab, click the **Format** tab.
3. Under the **Text Box Styles** group, click one of the predefined overall styles or click the **More** list arrow at the right to see all the style choices; click the desired one.

To change the overall design of the entire document:

1. From the **Page Layout** tab, in the **Themes** group, point to the **Themes, Colors, Fonts,** or **Effects** buttons as desired and watch the **Live Preview**.
2. Click the desired choice(s).

To edit the text in a text box when the insertion point is no longer inside the text box:

1. Click in the box to select it, and begin editing the text.

   Note: You may change the font or font color as desired.

2. When you are finished editing text, click outside the box to exit the text box.

(continued on next page)

PRACTICE *(continued)*

1. Insert a text box in the bottom half of the page about 4 inches wide and 2 inches high.
2. Click inside the text box, change to Arial Bold 28 point, press **ENTER** 1 time, and center and type Sun Industries.
3. Press **ENTER** 1 time, and in Arial Bold 16-point, center and type 759 Wilshire Boulevard.
4. Press **ENTER** 1 time, and in Arial Bold 16-point, center and type Los Angeles, CA 90017.
5. Insert a picture of the sun, and change the text wrapping style to **In Front of Text**.
6. Drag and position the text box and picture as desired or use the illustration under the last step as a model.
7. Change the outline, fill, or overall style of the text box to coordinate with the picture as desired. Change any fonts as desired.
8. You may arrange your finished document similar to the one in the illustration or design it as desired.
9. Your document should look similar to this:

Textbook

10. Save changes to *practice-103*, and return to GDP.

Designing Notepads

Print Options

When you are ready to print, you have several options. To see the available print options, click the **Microsoft Office Button**, point to **Print**, and three options will display.

Note: You will also see **GDP** as a choice under the **Microsoft Office Button** when you access Word via GDP.

Print allows you to select a printer, enter the number of desired copies, and other options. **Quick Print** sends all pages of the document directly to the default printer. **Print Preview** allows you to see how your page(s) will look when printed. On the keyboard, you can press press **CTRL + P** to go directly to the **Print** dialog box.

Note: For easier access to printing options, you can add buttons to the **Quick Access Toolbar**. Right-click any of the buttons and you will see options to add them to the **Quick Access Toolbar**.

You can choose to print on a specified number of pages or to a specified paper size. For example, if you have created a 4-page document such as the notepad illustrated on page 168 and you wanted all four pages to print on one sheet of paper, you would select 4 pages from the **Pages per sheet** drop-down list. If you wanted the four pages to print on a paper size other than letter size, you would select the desired choice from the **Scale to paper size** drop-down list. The four pages would be automatically scaled down and reduced to fit on the selected paper size.

(continued on next page)

To access print options:

1. Click the **Microsoft Office Button**, point to **Print**, and click **Print** in the right pane.

   Or: On the keyboard, press **CTRL + P**.

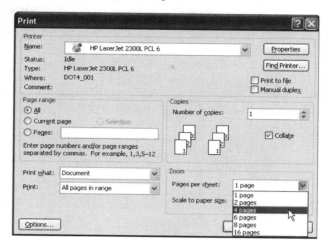

Note: Changes to print options are not saved for future printing.

2. Click the down arrow to open the **Pages per sheet** drop-down list. Click the desired number of pages to print per sheet of paper.
3. Click the down arrow to open the **Scale to paper size** drop-down list. Click the desired scaling option.

Note: If your pictures or text boxes won't print, you may need to adjust your print settings. Click the **Microsoft Office Button**, click **Word Options**; from the **Word Options** left pane, click **Display**; under **Printing** options, check **Print drawings created in Word**; click **OK**.

Note: If you have pictures and text boxes on the page, you might need to anchor them to a paragraph mark formatting symbol in order to copy and paste one page to create duplicate pages. To anchor an object such as a text box or picture, do this: Display formatting marks by turning on **Show/Hide**. Click the edge of the object to select it. You will see an anchor mark in the left margin area. Drag and drop the anchor to the first blank line at the top of the page or any desired spot. If you delete the line to which the object is anchored, you will also delete the object.

(continued on next page)

PRACTICE

Note: Check with your instructor before printing.

1. Display formatting marks by turning on **Show/Hide**.
2. Anchor all objects to the first blank line at the top of the page.
3. Change to a whole-page view, and select the entire document by pressing **CTRL + A** and copy the entire document by pressing **CTRL + C**.
4. Move to the end of the document by pressing **CTRL + END** and insert three manual page breaks by pressing **CTRL + ENTER** 3 times to create three additional blank pages.
5. Paste the copied document into each of the three newly created pages by moving the insertion point just before each manual page break formatting code and then pasting.
6. Scroll down to the end of this document. Note that it is four pages long and that each page is identical.
7. Use the print option to print four pages per sheet on 8.5- by 11-inch paper.

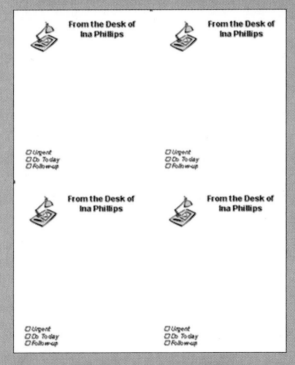

 Textbook

8. Save changes to *practice-104*, and return to GDP.

Designing Cover Pages

WordArt

WordArt is a drawing tool used to create special effects with text. A **WordArt** object can be formatted, rotated, realigned, and stretched to predefined shapes. The color and fill of the **WordArt** object can also be changed.

To insert a **WordArt** object:

1. From the **Insert** tab, **Text** group, click the **WordArt** button; then click the desired style from the **WordArt** gallery.

WordArt button

WordArt gallery

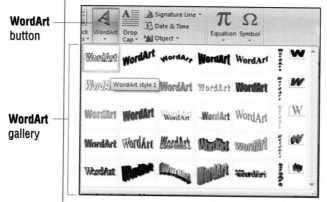

2. Type your text in the **Edit WordArt Text** dialog box.

3. Choose the desired font and font size for the text, and click **OK**.

Note: To edit text in your **WordArt**, right-click the **WordArt** object and click **Edit text**.

(continued on next page)

The **WordArt** object is inserted in the document and a **WordArt Tools** tab appears with a **Format** tab below it.

From the **WordArt Tools Format** tab, click on the various tools and experiment freely with all features:

1. From the **Arrange** group, click the **Text Wrapping** button and click **In Front of Text** to drag the WordArt freely.
2. In the **WordArt Styles** group, click the list arrow to view other gallery styles; point to each style, look at the **Live Preview**, then click the desired style to change it.
3. In the **WordArt Styles** group, click the **Shape Fill**, **Shape Outline**, and **Change Shape** buttons to change fills, outlines, and shapes. Look at the **Live Preview** as you point, then click the desired choice.
4. From the **Shadow Effects** and **3-D Effects** groups, click the different effects buttons to see what happens to your **WordArt** object.
5. From the **Size** group, experiment with the arrows next to the boxes to change sizes or drag on the size handles on the **WordArt** object.

PRACTICE

To create and format a WordArt object:

1. From the **Insert** tab, **Text** group, click the **WordArt** button; then click the desired style from the **WordArt** gallery.
2. Type Employee, press **ENTER**, and type Benefit Plan; choose a font and click **OK**.
3. Drag the **WordArt** object to the top of the page until it is positioned approximately as shown in the illustration.
4. From the **WordArt Tools Format** tab, experiment freely with all features.
5. You may arrange your finished document similar to the one in the illustration or design it as desired.

(continued on next page)

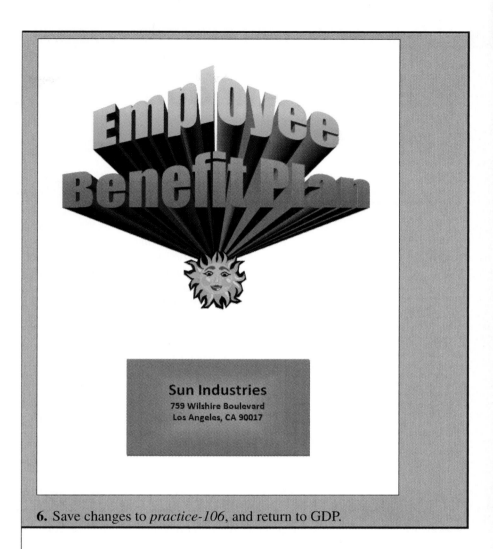

Go To Textbook

6. Save changes to *practice-106*, and return to GDP.

Designing Announcements and Flyers

Table—Move

Table move handle

Mouse pointer positioned on top of table move handle.

The easiest way to move a table is to point to the table until the **table move handle** appears just above the top left-hand corner of Cell A1, and then click the **table move handle.**

Use the **Table Tools Design** tab groups to add overall styles and designs to your table. Experiment freely with the features in all these groups: **Table Style Options**, **Table Styles**, and **Draw Borders**. Use the **Live Preview** feature to help you make good design choices.

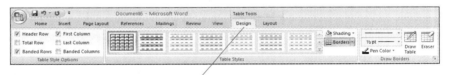

Table Tools Design tab groups

To move a table:

1. Place the mouse pointer over the table until the **table move handle** appears.
2. Point to the **table move handle** until a four-headed move arrow appears.
3. Drag the table to the new location.

Note: Switch to **Print Layout** view or reduce the **Zoom** level if necessary for a better view of the table position on the page.

(continued on next page)

PRACTICE

1. Move the mouse pointer over the table until you see the **table move handle**.

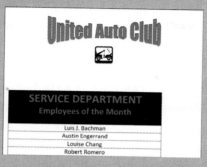

2. Drag the table until the table is positioned approximately as shown in the illustration.

Textbook

3. Click inside the table and use the **Table Tools Design** tab groups to add overall style and design to your table.
4. Save *practice-107*, and return to GDP.

Creating, Saving, and Viewing Web Pages

Web Page—Creating and Saving

Word can save documents as Web pages by converting them to HTML (Hypertext Markup Language), a file type that can be published to the Internet. HTML code tells a Web browser such as Microsoft Internet Explorer how to display and format a Web page with text and pictures. When you save a page as a **Single File Web Page (*.mht; *.mhtml)**, Word saves your document (and any pictures or formatting you added) as a Web page but generates only one file. When a file is saved as a **Single File Web Page**, several things happen:

- In the **Save As** window in the **Save as type** box, note that the file name extension changes from **Word Document (*.docx)** to **Single File Web Page (*.mht; *.mhtml)**.
- Because Web pages display text in the browser's title bar, you should add a short, descriptive title to the Web page when it is saved. Click the **Change Title** button to add or change a page title.

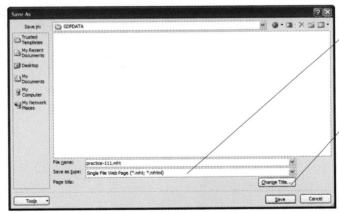

Note that **Single File Web Page (*.mht; *.mhtml)** is displayed as the file format.

Click the **Change Title** button to change the title of the Web page as it will be displayed in a browser.

(continued on next page)

Web Layout view button

- Note that the document view changes to **Web Layout**. Text wraps to fit the window size rather than being controlled by margins.
- Note that objects are positioned similar to what they would be in a Web browser.

To save a document as a **Single File Web Page (*.mht; *.mhtml)** wih a title:

1. Click the **Microsoft Office Button**, and click **Save As**.
2. After the **Save As** window appears, click the list arrow in the **Save in** box to browse to the desired folder.
3. Click the list arrow in the **Save as type** box, and click **Single File Web Page (*.mht; *.mhtml)**.

Note: The display of file extensions is controlled by Windows. Depending on your system setup, you may or may not see file extensions.

4. Click the **Change Title** button, type the desired title, and click **OK**.
5. Type the desired file name in the **File name** box, and click **Save**.

Note: Do not type the period or the *mht* extension after the file name—Word will add them automatically. Use hyphens in place of spaces in the file name or the page may not display properly in some browsers.

To change a Web page title:

1. Open the Web page.
2. Click the **Microsoft Office Button**, and click **Prepare**, **Properties**.
3. From the **Properties** window, **Summary** tab, click in the **Title** box; change the title as desired, and click **OK**.

(continued on next page)

PRACTICE

Note: Complete the Practice exercises in order. Do not skip or change the sequence of Lessons 111–115.

1. Observe the following for *practice-111.docx* as a Word document (*.docx): The **Print Layout** view button to the left of the horizontal scroll bar is active; note the line ending for the text wrapping in the first line; and note that the table appears centered between the margins. You will compare your observations in this step with step 4.
2. Save the file as a **Single File Web Page** named *practice-111*, and change the title to practice-111. Do **not** type the extension (.mht)—it is automatically added.
3. Center the table horizontally.
4. Observe the following for *practice-111.mht* as a Web page: the **Web Layout** view button next to the horizontal scroll bar is now active; the text wrapping in the first line has changed; and the table is centered.

Note: Keep this document open, and continue reading.

Web Page—Viewing

Tables provide the "framework" for a Web page. By placing text and pictures inside table cells, you can exercise some control over margins, picture position, and white space when the page is viewed in a Web browser. Empty cells are often used in the layout of a Web page to visually separate table information.

Note: Always insert pictures with **Text Wrapping** set to **In Line With Text** so that you can use the alignment buttons on the Formatting toolbar to position the pictures. See Lesson 83 for additional information about text wrapping.

Web Layout view is used to design a Web page. (Refer to the illustrations of the finished practice exercises on page 177.) In **Web Layout** view, open tables will display with light blue gridlines. To view your page in a Web browser, you use **Web Page Preview**. Note that in **Web Page Preview**, table gridlines are not visible and line endings may vary from those in **Web Layout** view due to variations in monitor sizes, screen settings, and Web browsers. You do not need an Internet connection to use **Web Page Preview**, but you must have Web browser software installed.

(continued on next page)

Web Page Preview button added to **Quick Access Toolbar**

Web Layout view

Table gridlines are visible.

Line endings are fixed.

To preview a Web page in a browser, you need to first add the **Web Page Preview** command to the **Quick Access Toolbar**:

1. Open the desired Word file.
2. Click the list arrow next to the **Quick Access Toolbar** and click **More Commands**.
3. With **Customize** selected in the left pane, click the list arrow in the **Choose commands from list** box in the right pane, and click **All Commands**.
4. Scroll down the list, and click **Web Page Preview**.
5. Click **Add** to add the command to the **Quick Access Toolbar**; click **OK**.

Page title

View in browser

Table gridlines not visible.

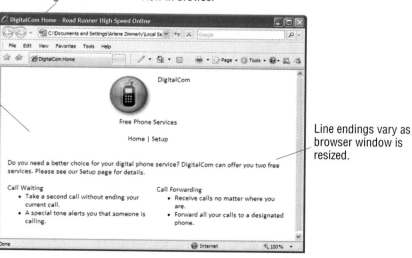

Line endings vary as browser window is resized.

(continued on next page)

PRACTICE *(continued)*

Note: Complete the Practice exercises in order. Do not skip or change the sequence of Lessons 111–115. *Practice-111.mht* should already be open from the previous practice exercise. Refer to the illustrations of the finished pages on page 177 as you complete the steps for this exercise.

1. Change the title from *practice-111* to `DigitalCom Home`.
2. Insert an empty row above and below the introductory paragraph.
3. Insert a row with 2 columns below the last row.
4. Type this sentence as the second bulleted item under the Call Waiting heading: `A special tone alerts you that someone is calling`.
5. Type this sentence as the second bulleted item under the Call Forwarding heading: `Forward all your calls to a designated phone`.
6. Click inside the empty cell in Row 1, and insert a picture of a phone. Verify that **Text Wrapping** is set to **In Line With Text**.
7. Size the picture to a height and width of about 1 inch, and align the picture at the right.
8. Observe your Web page in **Web Layout** view. It should look similar to the **Web Layout** view illustration on page 177. Note that table gridlines are visible. Also note the line endings in the first row of the table. You will compare your observations with **Web Page Preview** in the next step.
9. View the Web page in a browser. Note that table gridlines are not visible, note any changes in your line endings, and note the new page title in the title bar.
10. Close your browser, save *practice-111.mht*, and return to GDP.

Textbook

Creating Web Pages With Hyperlinks

Web Page—Hyperlinks

A hyperlink is an object (usually text or a picture) you click on to jump from one place to another. You might use a hyperlink to move within a Web page, to move to another Web page or Web site, or perhaps to open a different software program. Hyperlinked text usually displays underlined in a different color, and a hand icon appears when you mouse over the hyperlink.

To create a text hyperlink on a Web page:

1. Select the text for the hyperlink.
2. Right-click the selected text, and click the **Hyperlink** button. The **Insert Hyperlink** dialog box appears.

Insert Hyperlink button

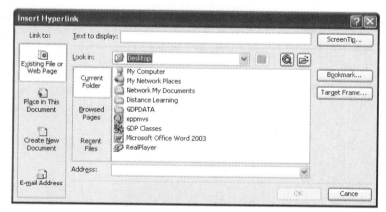

3. If necessary, under **Link to** on the left, click **Existing File or Web Page**.
4. If necessary, click the down arrow next to the **Look in** box, and browse to the desired directory.
5. Click the desired file name, and click **OK**.

Note: GDP has been set to u se relative hyperlinks (a hyperlink that points to the target file, but not to a specific location or directory for that file). Therefore, if you save your Web page to a different location such as a server, hyperlinks will not be broken. If you create Web pages outside of GDP, use these settings: Click the **Microsoft Office Button**, and click the

(continued on next page)

Word Options button at the bottom. In the **Word Options** window, from the left pane, click **Advanced**. Scroll down the right pane to the **General** area, and click **Web Options**. In the **Web Options** window from the **Files** tab, uncheck **Update links on save**. To ensure that hyperlinks are always relative, never copy and paste hyperlinks from one location to another.

To test the hyperlinks in Word:

1. With the desired Web page open in Word, click each hyperlink.

Note: If you click a hyperlink inside Word and nothing happens, do this: Click the **Microsoft Office Button**, and click the **Word Options** button at the bottom. In the **Word Options** window, from the left pane, click **Advanced**. In the right pane, under **Editing Options**, uncheck **Update links on save**. Click **OK**.

2. If the desired page appears, the hyperlink is correct.

Note: Hyperlinks cannot be reliably tested in a browser using **Web Page Preview**. Instead, point to the hyperlink and read the screen tip.

Inserting a hyperlink creates a hyperlink field (a field is a set of codes instructing Word to insert something into a document automatically). Pressing **ALT + F9** will display the field code itself so that you can verify that the target file is correct. For example, the home page for DigitalCom is shown in the illustrations with the hyperlink fields and then with the field codes displaying the hyperlink's target file.

To display hyperlink field codes:

1. Press **ALT + F9** to display the field code.
2. Press **ALT + F9** again to hide the field code.

To remove or edit a hyperlink:

1. Right-click on the hyperlink.
2. From the shortcut menu, click **Remove Hyperlink** or **Edit Hyperlink**, make the desired changes, and click **OK**.

(continued on next page)

NAVIGATING BETWEEN OPEN FILES

There are times when you will need to open, work on, and move to more than one file at a time. To navigate between open files:

1. Open the desired files.
2. From the **View** tab, **Window** group, click **Switch Windows**.
3. From the list of open files at the bottom, click the desired file.

PRACTICE

Note: Complete the Practice exercises in order. Do not skip or change the sequence of Lessons 111–115. Refer to the illustrations of the finished pages on pages 181 and 182 as you complete the steps for this exercise.

1. With *practice-113a.mht* open, also open *practice-113b.mht* and change the title to `DigitalCom Setup`.
2. Navigate back to *practice-113a*. Insert a text hyperlink on the link bar for *Home* and for *Services* to link to the corresponding Web pages (*practice-113a.mht* and *practice-113b.mht*).
3. Navigate to *practice-113b*. Insert a text hyperlink on the link bar for *Home* and for *Services* to link to the corresponding Web pages (*practice-113a.mht* and *practice-113b.mht*).
4. Test all the hyperlinks in Word, and edit any hyperlinks as needed.
5. Save and close *practice-113b*.
6. Save *practice-113a*, and return to GDP.

 Textbook

Practice-113a.mht

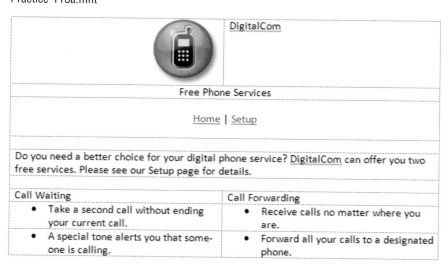

(continued on next page)

Practice-113b.mht

DigitalCom

Free Phone Services Setup

Home | Setup

DigitalCom offers you the two services described below free of charge. If you desire any additional services, we would be happy to assist you in making the right choice to fill your needs.

Setting Up Call Waiting
- Press and release the flash button when you hear the call waiting tone.
- Press the switchhook button again to switch between callers.

Setting Up Call Forwarding
- Life the receiver and press *72.
- When you hear a second tone, dial the number where your calls should be forwarded.
- When the phone is answered, hang up.

Formatting Web Pages

Web Page—Design Themes

A theme is a unified collection of design elements such as coordinated styles, themes, page backgrounds, fonts, and divider lines. Applying a theme to the pages in a Web site transforms it and provides unity and visual appeal.

If you apply styles to your headings before applying a theme, you will see a more noticeable change when you apply a theme. Styles should be used to make titles and headings consistent, distinctive, and "stylish." After you apply a theme and style, you might want to add a page background for more visual impact. You can also adjust font styles and colors as desired and add horizontal divider lines for visual separation of page content. Experiment freely, but be consistent from page to page.

To apply a style:

1. Select the desired text.
2. From the **Home** tab, in the **Styles** group, click the desired style; click the **More** button to see additional styles in the **Quick Styles** gallery.
3. Point to each style to see a **Live Preview** in your selected text or paragraph; then click the desired style.

Note: For a thorough review of styles, see Lesson 81.

To apply a theme:

1. Open the desired Web page with styles applied.
2. From the **Page Layout** tab, **Themes** group, click the **Themes** button.
3. Point to each theme, note the **Live Preview** on the Web page, and click the desired theme.

(continued on next page)

To add a page background:

1. Open the desired Web page with styles and theme applied.
2. From the **Page Layout** tab, **Page Background** group, click the **Page Color** button.
3. Point to each **Theme Color** or **Standard Color**, note the **Live Preview** on the Web page, and click the desired color.
4. From the **Page Layout** tab, **Themes** group, click the **Colors** button; point to various built-in colors and make any desired changes.

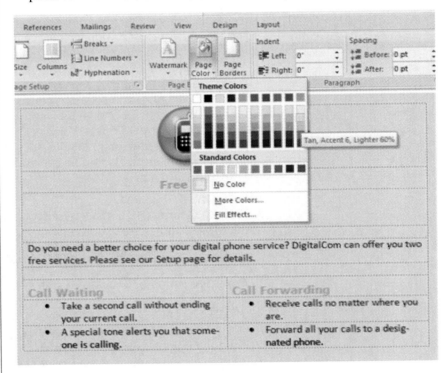

To adjust font colors:

1. Open the desired Web page with styles, theme, and page background applied.
2. From the **Page Layout** tab, **Themes** group, click the **Fonts** button.
3. Point to each built-in theme set of fonts, note the **Live Preview** on the Web page, and click the desired theme font.

To insert a horizontal line:

1. Open the desired Web page with styles, theme, page background, and font colors applied.
2. From the **Page Layout** tab, **Page Background** group, click the **Page Borders** button.

(continued on next page)

3. From the **Borders and Shading** window, **Page Border** tab, click the **Horizontal Line** button.
4. From the **Horizontal Line** window, click the desired line, and click **OK**.

PRACTICE

Note: Complete the Practice exercises in order. Do not skip or change the sequence of Lessons 111–115. Refer to the illustrations on page 186 as you complete the steps for this exercise.

1. If necessary, change the title of *practice-115a.mht*, the Home page, to `DigitalCom Home`.
2. Leave *practice-115a* open, create an additional new Web page named *practice-115b*, and, if necessary, change the title to `DigitalCom Setup`.
3. Insert the file *setup-115b.mht* into *practice-115b.mht*, the Setup page.

   Note: See Lesson 83, Insert a File, for a review of file insertion. When you insert *setup-115b.mht*, remember to change **Files of type** to **All Files (*.*).**

4. Verify that the hyperlinks in the link bars on both pages are set as follows: the Home link should point to *practice-115a.mht* and the Setup link should point to *practice-115b.mht*.
5. Test the hyperlinks in Word and edit them if needed.
6. Apply a **Heading 1** style to *DigitalCom* on the first line of the Home and Setup pages so that the business name is distinct.
7. Apply a **Heading 2** style to the heading in Row 2 on both the Home and Setup pages so that they display with a smaller font than the business name. Center the line if needed.
8. Apply a **Heading 3** style to the headings *Call Waiting, Call Forwarding, Setting Up Call Waiting,* and *Setting Up Call Forwarding* on both the Home and Setup pages.
9. Apply a desired theme, page background, and font color.
10. Insert a horizontal divider line in each blank row on both the Home and Setup pages.
11. View the Web pages in a browser, and make any desired changes to any part of the page design as desired. Your Web pages should look similar to the illustrations that follow these steps, although your colors, fonts, horizontal lines, etc., might be different.
12. When you are satisfied with all changes, save the files and close the browser.
13. Return to GDP.

Go To Textbook

(continued on next page)

Practice-115a.mht

DigitalCom

Free Phone Services

Home | Setup

Do you need a better choice for your digital phone service? DigitalCom can offer you two free services. Please see our Setup page for details.

Call Waiting
- Take a second call without ending your current call.
- A special tone alerts you that someone is calling.

Call Forwarding
- Receive calls no matter where you are.
- Forward all your calls to a designated phone.

Practice-115b.mht

DigitalCom

Free Phone Services Setup

Home | Setup

DigitalCom offers you the two services described below free of charge. If you desire any additional services, we would be happy to assist you in making the right choice to fill your needs.

Setting Up Call Waiting
- Press and release the flash button when you hear the call waiting tone.
- Press the switchhook button again to switch between callers.

Setting Up Call Forwarding
- Life the receiver and press *72.
- When you hear a second tone, dial the number where your calls should be forwarded.
- When the phone is answered, hang up.

Start Word From Windows

Microsoft Office Word icon on **Windows Start** menu

Microsoft Office Word icon on the **Windows Desktop** or **Windows Taskbar**

To start Microsoft Word from Windows:

1. If you have not done so, turn on your computer and start Windows.
2. On the **Start** menu, point to **Programs**, point to **Microsoft Office**, and click the **Microsoft Office Word 2007** icon as the Microsoft Office menu expands.

   Or: On the Windows desktop or on the Windows taskbar, double-click the Word icon.

3. If the Word icon is on the desktop, double-click to open Word. If it is in the Microsoft Windows shortcut bar, or if you access it from the **Start** button, click once to open Word.

   In a few seconds, Word displays its main screen with a blank document open ready for your input. The appearance of the screen depends upon the defaults that have been set for your computer and what settings were in effect when Word was last closed. Many features on the **Ribbon** and elsewhere in Word are dynamic (appear as needed) and change as features are used. See Lesson 21, Orientation to Word Processing—A, Start Your Word Processor for a detailed look at the Word window and its various parts.

(continued on next page)

Default settings are options that are in effect unless you specifically change them.

Word comes with some default settings that can change dynamically (as needed) as you use Word. In order to provide standardized, predictable settings as you work through the practice exercises and document processing jobs, GDP will automatically control certain settings. Default settings are any setting such as margins or fonts that are in effect automatically when Word is opened. See the Getting Started Section, GDP Default Settings, for details.

It is important to know what version of Word you are using for purposes of troubleshooting and technical support. To find out your Word version, when you launch Word and a new document opens, click the **Microsoft Office Button**, then click the **Word Options** button at the bottom of the pane. In the **Word Options** window, click **Resources**. Under **about Microsoft Word 2007**, you will see the version name and number. For more detail, click the **About** button. In the **About Microsoft Word window**, click **System Info . . .** for details about your computer specifications. Click **OK** and **Cancel** to exit.

Quit Word

Word Close button

To quit Microsoft Word:

1. On the title bar, click Word's **Close** button at the far right.

   Or: On the keyboard, press ALT + F4.
   If you have not saved your document, Word prompts you to save it.

A Brief Introduction to the Internet

Overview—What Is the Internet?

The Internet, also known as the *Net*, is a massive worldwide network of computers. Through the Internet, you can access information, conduct research, participate in discussion groups, play games, shop for just about anything, and send e-mail to friends, businesses, and family. The Internet is a valuable source on any topic. You can look at newspapers from anywhere in the world, read magazines, get tax forms and information on how to complete them, and even search for a job. You can also learn about worldwide events almost as soon as they happen.

Even the most farsighted Internet pioneers did not predict the enormous growth and the tremendous impact the Net has had on global communication. Experts even have difficulty calculating how many millions of people use the Internet daily from either their homes or their workplaces.

The Internet started in 1969, when the Advanced Research Projects Agency (ARPA) of the United States Department of Defense connected computers at different universities and defense contractors. The goal of the ARPANET was to build a network with multiple paths that would survive a disaster and to provide computing resources to users in remote locations. ARPANET expanded rapidly, and in the mid-1980s the National Science Foundation (NSF) created NSFnet to complement ARPANET. The link between ARPANET and NSFnet was the Internet. The Internet continued to grow as private companies developed their own networks and connected to the Internet through gateways. In 1990 the original ARPANET was discontinued. Today the Internet connects thousands of networks and millions of users.

The Internet is huge and has no central ownership. This means that no single person or group controls it. Specialized groups propose standards and guidelines for the appropriate use of the Internet. These organizations uphold the Internet's openness and lack of centralized control. This openness has attracted millions of users.

(continued on next page)

There are many ways to access the Internet, including connecting through a LAN (local area network), modem, or high-speed data link. To connect a desktop computer to the Internet, you need appropriate hardware and software. An Internet service provider (ISP) provides Internet software, and there is usually a monthly fee for Internet services. Be sure to shop around for your ISP because there are a variety of plans available. Estimate how many hours you will be using the Internet and then choose a plan that suits your needs.

How the Internet Works

Every computer on the Internet has a unique numeric address called an *Internet protocol address* (IP address). Most computers also have an address that uses words or characters in addition to the numeric address called a *domain name system* (DNS). DNS addresses have two parts, consisting of an individual name and a domain name. The chart shows popular domain names used in the United States. Domain addresses outside the United States use country codes in the domain name (example: .fr for France).

Internet Domains

Domain	Type of Organization	Example
.com	Business (commercial)	ibm.com (International Business Machines Corp.)
.edu	Educational	umich.edu (University of Michigan, Ann Arbor, MI)
.gov	Government	whitehouse.gov (The White House)
.mil	Military	navy.mil (The United States Navy)
.net	Gateway or host (or business/commercial)	mindspring.net (Mindspring, a regional Internet service provider)
.org	Other organization (typically nonprofit)	isoc.org (The Internet Society)

(continued on next page)

Internet Elements

The Internet has many elements and offers various services. Some of the most popular elements of the Internet include the World Wide Web, search engines, Web browsers, electronic mail (e-mail), newsgroups, and FTP—file transfer protocol.

The *World Wide Web* (WWW) is a graphical system on the Internet. A *Web site* is a location where an individual, a university, a government agency, or a company stores Web pages. These Web pages contain information about a particular subject. A Web site is a collection of related Web pages. A *hit* is the term used to indicate that someone has viewed a Web page. Popularity is determined by how many hits a Web page has accumulated. By clicking on a graphic or picture in the Web site, you may jump to a different Web page through the use of hypertext markup language (HTML). The hypertext links are the foundation of the World Wide Web.

Web browsers are used to find and view Web pages. You need to have a browser to access the World Wide Web and open the documents on your computer. Two of the most popular browsers are Microsoft Internet Explorer and Netscape Navigator. Web browsers gather resources from the Internet and put this information at your fingertips.

Electronic mail (e-mail) is the most commonly used Internet tool. With e-mail, people are able to communicate with friends, family, and coworkers anywhere in the world. You can create an address book to record frequently used e-mail addresses. You can send files as attachments with e-mail messages. Sending e-mails is easy, instant, and inexpensive.

Newsgroups are electronic bulletin board services on the Internet. There are thousands of newsgroups, and each is dedicated to a discussion of a particular subject. Anyone may post an article about the newsgroup's topic. You can read all the articles posted as well as see the initial entry that started the topic of discussion.

File transfer protocol (FTP) is an Internet tool used to copy files from one computer to another. A good example of the use of FTP is at tax time. You can access a government Web site and download information about taxes, including any forms you may need.

The Internet and You

In a short period of time, the Internet has become an integral part of school, home, and work. The Internet enhances our lives by offering new job opportunities, work-from-home offices, shopping for goods and services from anywhere (e-commerce), entertainment, and expanded research opportunities. It is an extraordinary communication tool. The Internet's reach and usefulness are limitless.